Robber Rocks

Letters and Memories of Hart Crane

Robber Rocks

Letters and Memories of
Hart Crane, 1923–1932

By SUSAN JENKINS BROWN

WESLEYAN UNIVERSITY PRESS
Middletown, Connecticut

Acknowledgment is gratefully made:

To Brom Weber for his permission to publish all the letters by Hart Crane included in this book, some of which were first published in full or in part in *The Letters of Hart Crane, 1916–1932,* originally published in a limited edition in 1952 by Hermitage House of New York City and reissued in a paperbound edition in 1965 by The University of California Press. Copyright 1952 by Brom Weber.

To *The Southern Review,* in the Autumn-1968 number of which a portion of this book was first published under the title "Hart Crane: The End of Harvest."

To *Venture,* in Volume 4: Number 1 of which "The Last Days of Hart Crane" by Peggy Baird was first published in 1961. Copyright © 1961 by Peggy Baird Conklin.

To Irving Caesar and to Warner Brothers-Seven Arts Music, Incorporated, for permission to reprint the lyrics of the song "What do you do Sunday, Mary?". Copyright 1923 by Harms, Incorporated.

For Jason Slater Brown
who, at the age of three, made the exciting
discovery that language is metaphor:
"Grandma! A feather is the leaf of a bird!"

Contents

Author's Note

A few misspellings, mistypings, accidental omission of a necessary word, and one misquotation have been corrected in this publication to avoid the use of *sic*. Hart Crane was an accurate typist and he rarely made errors in grammar, syntax and spelling even in hastily typed or penned letters meant only for the eyes of the recipient. Mr. Brom Weber used this policy in his readable edition of Crane's letters. For those readers whose aims are other than readability, almost all the original letters are available in major university libraries.

The letters in this collection were written between 1923 and 1932, to me (SJB), my former husband William Slater Brown (WSB), Malcolm Cowley (MC), his first wife Peggy Baird Cowley (PBC), and his second and present wife Muriel Cowley (Muriel C). Almost half of these letters have been published before, most only in excerpt. The remainder are here published for the first time. With the exception of *Letter #25*, the originals of the letters addressed to the Cowleys are in the Hart Crane Collection of the Yale University Library which, at the request of Mr. Cowley, kindly supplied me with verbatim reproductions for use in this book. With the exception of *Letter #18*, the originals of the letters addressed to me and William Slater Brown are in the Hart Crane Collection of the Columbia University Library. The original of *Letter #18* is in the Brown University Library. I am indebted to Mr. Kenneth Lohf, curator of Columbia's Special Collections, for giving me access to other Hart Crane materials.

I am deeply grateful to Mr. Donald E. Stanford, co-editor of *The Southern Review,* for his editorial suggestions.

Robber Rocks

Letters and Memories of Hart Crane

Letters and Memories of Hart Crane

In May or June of 1923 one of my friends brought Hart Crane to my flat at 30 Jones Street in New York City. It may have been Kenneth Burke or William Slater Brown, or both. Hart soon became a frequent visitor; I enjoyed his company.

In a letter to his mother from New York (June 10, 1923) Hart wrote: "Really, I'm having the finest time of my life. There's no use trying to describe the people I go around with. Last night, marketing with Sue and Bill down in the Italian section was a perfect circus. We carried pots and pans, spinach, asparagus, etc., from place to place. I've never been with young people I've enjoyed so much. Then there's Kenneth Burke up at *The Dial* office, Matty Josephson, Edward Nagle, Gaston Lachaise, Malcolm Cowley — but what's the use of going on with so many mere names. You can see how much fun I am having."

Malcolm Cowley was not, in fact, in New York City at that time; he and his wife Peggy Baird Cowley were then in Paris and did not return until August. Yet, in a deeper sense, Hart was not stretching a point very far in including him in this list, for he was in touch with Malcolm by correspondence, and knew that they would meet soon. They had met by mail through a review Hart had written of *Eight More Harvard Poets* for the March-April, 1923, issue of *S4N,* in which Hart had singled out for praise the poetry of two of the eight: Malcolm Cowley and John Brooks Wheelwright. Malcolm read the review in France and wrote to the reviewer:

> Giverny par Vernon, Eure
> May 20, 1923

Dear Crane: — Thanks for your note in *S4N* which I thought was the most intelligent criticism our book received. I hope I was right. Anyhow you gave me a chance to tell you that I like your own poems. For several months I have been telling people how good they are, and perhaps I have made some impression. You write with a bombast which is not Elizabethan but contemporary, and you are one of two or three people who can write a 20th Century blank verse, about other subjects than love, death and nightingales and in other patterns than ti tum ti tum ti tum ti tums. Salutations.

"Poster," in *Secession* #4 was printed between Williams and Stevens, and was far better than either of them. *O brilliant kids* is the most simple, the most brilliant combination of noun and epithet that I have seen these many years.

I hope you don't rush to print a volume. If we all wait three or four years, till our public is formed, we can have a great deal more fun by publishing.

Mrs. Cowley and I are sailing in a few weeks. We hope to meet you when we get back.

The address from which Malcolm had written this letter — Giverny par Vernon, Eure — was not the accidental choice of a visiting American. It was the address from which the founder of the school of French Impressionist painting, Claude Monet, had been addressing his letters since 1883, when he settled there with his large family. Malcolm had met Monet's stepgrandson, Jim Butler, when visiting my first husband, James Light, and me in our New York apartment at 86 Greenwich Avenue, our "Maison Clemenceau," after the French statesman, who had lived there during his years in exile in the late 1860s. Jim's mother, one of Monet's stepdaughters, had married an American pupil of Monet's, Theodore Butler. Jim had grown up in Giverny, and had learned to paint from Monet. After serving in the U.S. Army in World War I, he lived with his parents at 75 Washington Place in New York City and was a daily visitor at Maison Clemenceau. At that time he gave me one of his few paintings: an Impressionist study of a tree-draped pool in the Epte River at Giverny, signed "J Butler 1918." To me, it looks like a good Monet. Later Jim returned to Giverny where during the "American exile" period he often found rooms in the village for American friends. Malcolm and his wife Peggy were among them, also the Josephsons and Robert M. Coates.

Malcolm's friendship with Hart, begun through a shared interest in poetry, and in each other's poems, was to remain firm throughout Hart's life. It helped to cement my own friendship with Hart. When I met him Hart was the guest of his old friend, Gorham Munson, while looking for a job and a room of his own.

Away from his home in Cleveland, with his mother and father divorced, Hart was soon to adopt me and a number of my friends as his family. Besides the Cowleys and the Burkes, there were William Slater Brown (later, my husband), Allen and Caroline Tate, Matthew and Hannah Josephson, Bina Flynn and her husband Romolo Bobba. Eleanor Fitzgerald, then the business manager of the Provincetown Players, and Emil Opffer were soon added. Of these friends, old and new, Hart had met Josephson during an earlier stay in New York City in 1919, when he had roomed above the *Little Review* office on West 16th Street. He had kept up a correspondence with him from Cleveland, in which he mentioned his interest in the writings of Kenneth Burke, whom he knew to be a friend of Matty's. Allen Tate he had also met by correspondence, which started through their contributions in the same issue of *Double Dealer*. Hart's was a translation of Jules Laforgue's *Locu-*

tions des Pierrots; Allen's a poem that interested Hart so much he wrote the poet a letter of praise. This was in May of 1922. It started a long-continued literary correspondence and, after a year or so, a close friendship.

My flat at 30 Jones Street was a convenient meeting place for this group. Hart, being a loner, was there most frequently — so often that a few persons thought he lived there. He never did. The flat was a spacious old-fashioned "through floor," on the parlor level of a three-story red-brick house, looking out onto a pleasant rear garden. Hart was a general favorite there. The qualities that he displayed in his letters were also in his conversation; he was perceptive, witty, articulate, and often eloquent. Still devoted to his mother and missing her, he was given to talking about her to his new women friends. He looked forward to having her meet us. "You'll love each other," he would say to each of us. "She's so lovely, you can't help it. And she'll adore you."

I sympathized with Hart's need of friends for I, too, had been lonely when I first moved into Jones Street in the fall of 1922. I had just started the slow process of a divorce from Jimmie Light, after five years of marriage. Early in 1922, Jimmie had quite suddenly told me that he intended to go to France, for an indefinite stay. He told me his reason for doing so. He hoped I would be patient and wait to see how "things turned out." I was crushed, but I let him go, though I made no promise as to patience. Then I disposed of our apartment on Bedford Street and went to live with Johanne Boving until my spring-season work with the Provincetown Players was ended. I was then the Players' secretary, assistant to Fitzi in the box office, and reader of unsolicited plays, which came in daily by the dozen. George Cram Cook, the Players' founder, retired to Greece at this time, and the Players decided to close for the 1922–1923 season. Through Fitzi, I established a Connecticut residence as a first step toward a divorce for desertion. That summer I was the guest of my old friend Blanche Hays (Mrs. Arthur Garfield Hays) in Woodstock. In the fall the resourceful Blanche found a job for me as editor of a pulp magazine,

Telling Tales. Another friend, Lorna Dietz, turned over to me the Jones Street flat that she was vacating. With such helpful friends, I was able to re-shape my life.

Early in 1923, Jimmie came back to New York, unhappy, broke, and very clinging. It was too late; our marriage had ended for me, though not our friendship. He bunked with the painter, Harry Gottlieb, in a basement room in Patchin Place, coming to eat at Jones Street when he wasn't invited elsewhere. Soon he got a job stage-managing a touring play and was away from New York until the fall of 1923, when he returned to directing plays for the Provincetown, revitalized by Gene O'Neill and Robert Edmond Jones. He did not return to marital life with me, however; for the time being, I was through with marital life. Hart was then a frequent visitor at Jones Street, as was Jimmie for some months. But Hart and Jimmie were never to become close friends — possibly because Jimmie was rarely on the New York scene in the early Twenties, for he was off to Europe again in early 1924, in charge of the touring company of *Emperor Jones.* After my move to Robber Rocks, Hart and Jimmie rarely saw each other, though Jimmie gave whole-hearted support to the publication of *White Buildings.* Hart's letters play up Jimmie somewhat, just as they do O'Neill and Charlie Chaplin; he needed "known names" to reassure his mother, father and Cleveland friends as to how he was getting on in New York — a forgivable exaggeration.

When Bill Brown and I married and moved to an old farmhouse in Dutchess County in New York, Hart promptly asked if he could join us there to help fix it up. He soon became a part of the place. Some of our son Gwiffy's first understandable words were "good old Hart." He had seen Hart carrying in logs for the fireplace or water from the well, or Hart with my apron around him washing dishes. When Hart said, "Let me wash the dishes," he meant it. After one long spell of dishwashing at the Cowleys he told Caroline Tate: "I washed dishes until the cloth fell from my nerveless fingers."

But the most vivid memory is of Hart laughing — laughing so that the little boy and all around him would irresistibly join in.

There was a darker side to this simple life in the country, especially after the bitter quarrel with his mother early in 1928. But even in the depressions and miseries of his last two years he never entirely lost his amiable qualities. Later biographers and commentators, not knowing Hart Crane, have stressed this darker aspect, it seems to me — a few of them to the neglect of all else, perhaps misled by some who *did* know him. Tantrums and violence can so readily be recalled that they tend to blur recollections of more admirable but less dramatic elements. One can recall the sensation of spontaneous joy and laughter, but not often can one reproduce the wit and humor that provoked it. Hart's letters are far better witnesses to his life than the best-intentioned of his friends. The man who in such a short span wrote a large body of distinguished poetry was not an abandoned debauchee eleven months a year, as one conscientious writer was misled into seeing him. He *could* not have been, not even during the last two years; there was not time for it. Even toward the end, he never completely gave up the struggle against his two weaknesses, alcohol and homosexuality.

During his disastrous stay in California in 1928, he seems to have lost his ability to "tolerate" alcohol; from that time on, complete abstinence was the only alternative, though a hard one for him, as it has been for others. His longing for a satisfying way of living, his urge to produce and to create, enabled him to make the rational choice and to stick to it long enough to do thoughtful reading and to write some poetry. Yet such is alcoholism that these months of sane living could not recover lost ground. In his last year or so a resumption of drinking would, within a few hours, reduce him to the lowest level that he had previously reached and then plunge him even lower.

As to his homosexuality, I am not alone in thinking that his reports exaggerated it — just as in his earlier years he told exaggerated stories of his behavior when intoxicated, out of braggadocio and to get his tale in first before somebody else told it about him. If Hart Crane had chosen to conceal his homosexual inclination, I doubt that even his close friends would have suspected it. He seemed to be a normal male. The reasons for his not concealing it are, to me, obscure and complex. He avoided homosexual groups and individuals, having a distinct antipathy to them. "I never liked falsetto" is the way he put it. His social life was spent with heterosexuals, most of them married and with children. He felt free to introduce an occasional new or old friend into the social group of which I was a part, but I cannot recall one homosexual among them. As his letters show, and as his friends knew, he had an unusual capacity for friendship. Once he had become an intimate part of our social group, he sought us out almost daily. Allen Tate has described Hart Crane as an extreme example of the unwilling homosexual.

These remarks are made not with the thought that they throw much light on the alcoholism and homosexuality of Hart Crane, but with the desire to avoid repetition of these subjects, whenever possible, in the uncensored presentation of the letters that follow. A primary purpose is to make available heretofore unpublished letters written by Hart Crane to William Slater Brown and me, and to give the full versions of those letters that have been published only in part in *The Letters of Hart Crane: 1916–1932*.*

Adding immeasurably to the interest and value of this memoir is the inclusion here of the letters that Hart wrote to Malcolm Cowley, which cover the same period as the letters to us. This correspondence brings out a different facet of Hart's temperament, rounding out the picture. A number of these letters have not been published before. In them is revealed an interesting and, I believe, unique epi-

*The Letters of Hart Crane: 1916–1932. Brom Weber, editor. New York City: Hermitage House, 1952. Paperback edition: Univ. of Cal. Press. 1965.

sode in American literary life: Hart's aid to Malcolm in assembling and arranging the poems that were to become Malcolm's first volume of collected poems *Blue Juniata*† — even down to the drudgery of typing and retyping the poems. At my request Malcolm has written a note about this episode. All comments on the Cowley letters are by me.

Obscure references in both sets of letters are clarified. A biographical background is supplied by relating, more or less chronologically, the pertinent events in Hart Crane's life at the time the letters were written and between letters: those events that the letters do not relate but which add to their interest and meaning. About half the letters have not been published before. Initials identify the recipients.

Letter #1.   To SJB.   From Woodstock, New York.   November 13, 1923

Dear Sue:

Bill probably writes you all the news worth telling right along, so I'll desist. I have meant to write you much sooner, though, just as a matter of contact with you, the compliments of the excursion, etc. Life is very pleasant here, despite all the guests that we have been having, and it is no less arduous. My biceps are larger and my cheeks are much bekindled, but as for TIME — His shoulders are more narrowed than the spirit of the necktie counter's tender on a Jan. evening. I have not had a moment to do the three briefers for the *Dial* that I took up here as a precautionary measure. Letters likewise. Meanwhile the fireplace glitters and the stove consumes, and we eat enormous meals. The joyful little s-s of b-tches of villanelles that I was going to write for

†*Blue Juniata,* poems by Malcolm Cowley. New York: Jonathan Cape & Harrison Smith: 1929.

Blue Juniata, Collected Poems, by Malcolm Cowley, was published last year by The Viking Press and includes the poems of the earlier volume and those written since, the latest, "The Flower and the Leaf," being a reminiscence of Hart Crane.

you are still in an orphaned purgatory, so let us pray!

Please don't bother too much about that room therefore, Sue. I am very likely, as I see things now, to be back there in full glory next month. Otherwise it will be easy enough to move my things into storage and return here. Wherever I am, I must get some time to earn a tiny sum, and my reason for the room mention, as you will guess, is pretty well covered by the outlook here in that particular of time. Certainly nothing else would move me in a thousand years. Bill and Nagle are paragons of affability and entertainment and I like the mountain air.

Jimmy writes that Gene is in town and that his brother died. This doesn't call for conventional expressions, but I wish you would give Gene and Agnes my ripest salutations. There was no end of fun and celebration at my Ridgefield visit.

Write me if you have time,
as always, hart

A young female cousin of mine from Canton, Ohio, has just arrived in N.Y. to find a job. She has worked on a newspaper, and may still be a virgin, for all I know. (Still, she has been to Smith!) I thought you might not mind talking to her a few minutes and have suggested that she calls at your office some day soon. I hope you won't mind giving her a little advice of some kind or other — all advice from you is good. Too damned sensible, as you have heard me complain!   h

Herr Rector is still with us! I'll be glad when either he gets his damned kerosene fliv going, or else it blows him into Norway.

Elizabeth Smith is the girl's name. She is living now at 20 Jones St. My regards to Jim, Emil and Rossberg(?). I might think of sailing off with them on their next trip south. I'm still tired of polite occupations. The candle has upset again.

The setting. — William Slater Brown and his friend Edward Nagle had rented an old farmhouse near the art colony at Woodstock in the Catskills from the family of Nagle's friend Anne Rector, a painter. Nagle, too, was a painter and the stepson of the sculptor Gaston Lachaise. Bill and Nagle had gone there early in the fall, prepared to stay through the severe Catskill winter. His nerves exacerbated by his copywriting job at J. Walter Thompson, which he called a "damned hypocrisy," Hart resigned and joined Bill and Nagle in Woodstock. Before deciding on this move he had planned to go to his grandmother's villa on the Isle of Pines near Cuba, but his mother told him that the villa was up for sale. Hart left New York City on November 1 with Malcolm and Peggy Cowley. Enroute to Woodstock, they stopped several days at Eugene O'Neill's country house in Ridgefield, Connecticut.

"Villanelles": I was then editing a pulp-paper love-story magazine named *Telling Tales,* and frequently filled out a page with an innocuous poem, for which we paid $10. I armed Hart with samples of our villanelles, but Hart's never emerged from their "orphaned purgatory." The dashes in this sentence are Hart's, for he was writing to a woman — a comment on the change in standards since 1923, when Hart Crane was not regarded as "a Nice Nelly." He was less scrupulous in his letters to men.

"Please don't bother about that room, Sue" — Hart had asked me to sub-sublet his room-and-bath at 45 Grove Street to save him the $25 monthly rent. The room was in an old, partly renovated mansion, reputed to have been the former town house of the Ogden Reid family, then owned by the ubiquitous Signora Bellardi, landlady to half of Greenwich Village, including the Provincetown Players on Macdougal Street, of which Jimmie Light was a director and where I, too, had been a working member of the group for several years. Other tenants at 45 Grove were Eleanor Fitzgerald, Stark Young, the drama critic, and Howard Scott the Technocrat. At the time of Hart's letter Malcolm and I had already installed Kenneth Burke there, as Malcolm said on a postcard to Hart dated November 28:

Of course the advantage of living in New York is the fact that one is so chronically busy that one does not think, or if one thinks, does not feel. Sometimes in a sudden rush of emotion you discover yourself to be bored, sad, violently good humored. The little stenographer asked me — Mr. Cowley, what is a *triste* — you know, an *engineering triste*. Before I could explain that she meant a treatise, the tears suddenly fell. Did you succeed in writing sexy stories? Woodstock seems distant and paradisial. Kenneth has taken your room, installed himself and Corona, and seems determined to write at any cost.

So was I — how long ago?

Malcolm was then working for *Sweet's Architectural Catalogue.* The annual edition was going to press, and he had no time to write anything but specifications for building materials.

A few days earlier, I had paid a flying visit to Woodstock, driving up with Agnes O'Neill from the O'Neills' "Brook Farm" in Ridgefield. I had forgotten this incident until it was brought back to memory by reading Agnes's obituary in the *Times* in 1968. Jimmie had induced me to go with him to Brook Farm where he had to see Gene, to get him to approve or change the final production script of *S.S. Glencairn,* the title given to an arrangement of O'Neill's one-act sea plays which the Players were to produce that season. We knew that Gene had not yet pulled out of the "binge" on which he had started when Hart and the Cowleys were at Brook Farm early in November, and our stay there turned out to be as distressing as I had feared. Gene had retired to a basement room of his large manor house with old Terry Carlin and three large casks of seasoned hard cider as companions. Jimmie had to sit there on an empty barrel with his working manuscript on a clipboard, extracting comments from Gene as best he could, and running upstairs to join Agnes and me at meals, to beg for our patience and to collect sandwiches for Gene and Terry. A day or so of this gloom and doom was all that I could stand. So with Jimmie's approval, early one morning Agnes and I started out for a drive on a beautiful fall day, taking a lunch basket. Agnes was fond of Hart, and we headed for Woodstock, hoping for a little gaiety. As we got out of the car and hallooed, Hart came running to meet us and rushed us out of the November chill to the warmth of the fireplace, where Bill and Nagle were placing chairs. Hart asked, "To what do we owe this great and unexpected pleasure?" Agnes replied, "Why, we came to see *you*." "Hooray!" Hart shouted. "Two lovely ladies drive sixty miles just to see me!" He seized Agnes and whirled her about so vigorously that bone hairpins sprinkled the floor and her roll of long, light-brown hair fell on her shoulders. Bill sat us down; Nagle brought us glasses of cider; I set out our basket lunch; Hart picked up the hairpins; and Agnes rearranged her hair. "I came to call on a gentle poet," she said, hairpins in her teeth, "and I run into a tropical hurricane." "But my poetry is for *all* seasons, including hurricanes" was his reply.

"Don't turn any more neat phrases," I cautioned Agnes, "or you'll meet them wherever you go. Hart is as good as a press agent for his friends' jokes." I went on to tell of an incident that had occurred recently. I was putting dinner on the table at 30 Jones Street while Hart read aloud from a newspaper an item reporting that medical tests showed that carbon monoxide in the exhaust of automobiles tended to make women sterile and men impotent. My comment was: "So now our culture calls upon us to sacrifice our virility on the altar of motion." Hart put down his paper and slapped his knee, laughing. "Sue, you're wonderful! So neat — so apt! On the altar of motion." He spread my small *mot* everywhere.

How good to hear laughter again, to see friendly, smiling faces! But we could indulge in little more than one warming hour in order to return by daylight. Meanwhile the news of our absence had penetrated to the Ridgefield cider cellar. When we drove up to the entrance, we could see Gene hovering in the front door, while Jimmie rushed out to the car. "Thank God you're back, both of you! I was afraid you had really run away. Gene's in a terrible state. Do, please, take it easy with him." The culprits marched into the hall to face Gene, who managed to twitch a rather sour grin in my direction. Before he could do more than turn his fierce Black Irishman's frown on Agnes, we ran upstairs to her room, leaving Gene to Jimmie's handling. But it didn't turn out too bad. Gene joined us for dinner that evening. His levees in the cider cellar had ended.

I have been wondering who supplied that obituary to the *Times*. What "friend" of O'Neill's could it have been who reported to the obit.-writer that the O'Neills' "home in New Jersey, as well as later ones in Bermuda and Maine, always seemed to smell of diapers and lamb stew and there was always a lot of noise from the kids. It drove O'Neill almost out of his mind." First-hand sniffing and hearing are implied, yet their winter's stay in Agnes's house in Point Pleasant, New Jersey, when they were poor and Gene had no other home to offer, occurred when there were no kids. After that there was always a fair amount of affluence, and Shane and Oona were strictly segregated. Agnes's little girl by a former marriage was brought up by Agnes's mother, and was permitted to pay only short visits, during which she was kept away from Gene. Jimmie hero-worshipped Gene, but he also loved children; he was deeply disturbed by Gene's stiffness toward Shane, a charming, active boy.

There are other mementos from Hart's brief stay in Woodstock; no wonder he hadn't been able to turn his attention to villanelles. He wrote a dozen or so letters, some quite long, and made a thorough revision of "Recitative," written just before he left New York City for Woodstock. He also wrote, or rewrote, "Interludium" and "Possessions." All these were published in magazines during the next few months, probably without the fees that villanelles would have brought him from *Telling Tales*.

While there, he developed a vein for parody, chiefly to entertain his housemates and their guests. Among Bill's

papers is a yellowing sheet dating from Hart's Woodstock
period — a full page of Hart's neat typing, under the innocuous heading: "Of an Evening," and signed: "emulating
Estlin by H. C." — which is reproduced on the facing page.

Letter #2. To MC. From Woodstock, New York. December 10, 1923
Dear Malcolm:

Having been lured into buying a hunter's coat today it
looks as though I might stay out the winter here, especially
since there is a chance of taking charge of some stock on top
of the Overlook — a peak in whose shadow we have been
dwelling here. At least I'm strongly tempted, and would like
to try out loneliness amid hurricanes and drifts at the pleasant risk of only monthly or bi-monthly visits to the nether
world of common speech. But that's very embryonic yet.
Meanwhile it rains and we forego the tasks of lumbering,
etc. It rains, and rains again.

The gentle melancholy of your card was gracious and
welcome; reassuring to know that THE CITY is a little
away from me yet.

"I SHALL HAVE SPEECH WITH YOU IN BABY-
LON" would start a good poem, perhaps, were not Babylon so outspoken already. Meanwhile the much-vaunted
sexy stories refuse to be born. I draw pictures, cook, sweep
and masturbate the cats. (We have two, now, besides a female, I'm told, in the barn, who never comes near the
house, but who runs her little evenings very successfully on
the tillage that our inmates provide her.)

Are you still on the brink of poetry, or is your suicide
entirely satisfied? After all the strains that poor B. has just
suffered for our tulips and our chimleys — I feel that criticism is much the more doughty profession. Tell peggy
to swear both for me and by me.

yrs

hart

OF AN EVENING
PULLING OFF A LITTLE EXPERIENCE
(with the english language)

by

NIGHTS

EEEEEECCCUUUMMMMMIIINNNGGGSSS
(for short)

69

        wrists web rythms
and the poke-
      ,dot smile;
of Genevive
            talks
back

i KNew, kneW my feet
?go on) were an applesauce
               part
of yoU belching POCHETTEkeepit
upyou s,uede
ballbearing

        celery-grin

remind of-of la guerre

    UM
Trimvirate (creamed dancing bitches)
corking with Helene, (exactly you make)
my perpendicularly crowdedPOCKets

        smilepoke

,,besides:which
April has
a
word to say: classy (eh(!
while blundering fumbiguts gather   accu
rate little, O-SO masturbations in/
               to
fractions of heaven. Hold tight   bless
worms trilling rimple flock to
sad iron
        goats of
      love-
        semi-colon
         piping (dash)

                    emulating
                     Estlin
                  by H. C.

23

Comment: Hart omits mention of his literary productions, perhaps because his pride at being able to cook, sweep, and saw wood is greater. *Tulips and Chimneys* (1923) was the title of E. E. Cummings' first collection of poetry, of which Slater Brown had just sweated out a review for the November issue of *Broom.* It is likely that Hart wrote his parody of Cummings while this was going on. Bill is the "B." or "WSB" in Cummings' *The Enormous Room.* During World War I they were both volunteers in the Norton-Harjes Ambulance Service, and they were both jailed (in "the enormous room") on suspicion of being pro-German, partly because they grew mustaches and were not very neat, partly because they spoke French and preferred the company of the French *poilus* to that of the other Americans.

Hart's impractical plan to winter alone on the top of inaccessible Overlook Mountain did not materialize. By early January Hart was back in his room at 45 Grove Street, "having speech in Babylon" with me and others. Several months later, however, Louis Kantor, the primary tenant of this room, returned from Europe, and Hart had to move to a more expensive and less pleasing furnished room on Charles Street, in a block officially named Van Nest Place for a time. Early in April, with the help of Emil, he shifted again, this time to the room at 110 Columbia Heights in Brooklyn, which he retained for some years.

After his return from Woodstock Hart became again a frequent dinner guest at 30 Jones Street. He and I often went together in the evenings to attend rehearsals and performances at the Provincetown Players nearby on Macdougal Street, especially when Jimmie Light was directing Strindberg's *Spook Sonata* and a dramatic version of Coleridge's *The Ancient Mariner,* which had been arranged by Eugene O'Neill and was played in masks designed by Jimmie. Hart begged Jimmie for casts of two of the masks, one for his Cleveland friends, the Rychtariks, and one for himself. At the end of the run he was given one of a drowned sailor, which he kept and displayed in his room, and another of an angel, which he sent to the Rychtariks. "The effect is unearthly," he wrote them. "You can have some fun playing with it in pantomine."

Early in February of 1924, Hart took me to a "demonstration" at the Neighborhood Playhouse on the Lower East Side, given by pupil-disciples of G. I. Gurdjieff, himself a disciple or a colleague of P. D. Ouspensky, the Russian philosopher and author of *Tertium Organum*. We witnessed "astonishing dances and psychic feats," as Hart later described them, in which some of our acquaintances were performers. Gurdjieff had a vogue in New York at that time among those engaged in a spiritual "search"; one still hears of adherents to the movement. Hart and I were irreverent but well-behaved, even at the sight of Mr. Gurdjieff visible from our sixth-row seats standing in the wings dressed in a costume resembling that of a lion-tamer. Occasionally he snapped above and around his bald brown head a long black whip, so strenuously that it made a loud "crack," a signal to his whirling pupils on the stage to remain rooted in their tracks. To the best of their ability they did, with only a little teetering; they were of all ages, sexes, and amplitudes. This, at any rate, is the picture engraved in my memory. The English critic A. R. Orage gave an interpretive talk that seemed to illuminate the converts but was less comprehensible to me. Hart found it "vague and arbitrary." Startlingly prominent in the well-filled auditorium were Margaret Anderson, editor of *The Little Review*, and her companion, Georgette LeBlanc, former wife of Maurice Maeterlinck — because they stood, side by side, in the third row with their backs to the stage most of the evening, facing the audience. Margaret was her usual handsome, tastefully dressed self, very pleasant to look at. But Georgette was got up in a peculiar, exotic style, especially as to make-up, which she had used to emphasize, rather than conceal, departures from the facial smoothness of youth — a decided contrast to the attractive "Martie," as Miss Anderson was called by her friends. Hart was so convulsed that he had to duck his head. "I won't dare say hello to Martie," he murmured, regaining control.

For some months Hart was largely dependent on a few friends, among whom he later named Gorham Munson, Stewart Mitchell (then on *The Dial*), Emil Opffer, and me — my share being to offer dinners at Jones Street. Malcolm Cowley finally got him a job as a copy-writer on *Sweet's Architectural Catalogue,* which he held from mid-April of 1924 until June of 1925. In that interval Allen Tate came to work as my assistant at *Telling Tales,* succeeding Hannah Josephson, who retired in time to give birth to a son.

It was a lively fall, winter, and spring for me and my friends, late 1924 and early 1925. We were all working, earning modest incomes, and most of us were without dependents. One could get a good Italian *table d'hote* for seventy-five cents or less; the Prohibition *vino rosso* was cheap and not *too* bad. Some ten or twelve of us had formed the practice of dining together fairly regularly every Saturday evening at John Squarcialupi's cheerful restaurant, at first in a large basement on Waverly Place, later on Perry Street. Our numbers were swelled by irregulars from time to time: Estlin and Ann Cummings, Bob and Elsa Coates, Harold Loeb (in New York temporarily to see his first novel *Doodab* through the press). Eleanor Fitzgerald sometimes joined us with Emil Opffer, during his year of editing *Nordlyset,* when he sublet half of Fitzi's large apartment at 45 Grove Street. We rarely knew in advance just who would turn up but, few or many, genial John Squarcialupi (the "Breaker of Wolves" we translated his name) always saw to it that tables were joined, and our quiet dining out would be turned into a gay, impromptu, Dutch-treat dinner party. At the end of the evening the onerous task of figuring out who owed what always fell to patient Malcolm Cowley. During the evening Hart invariably drifted over to an old upright piano to pound out his versions-by-ear of his favorite popular songs — a foot on the loud pedal, accentuating the pronounced rhythms, shaking his head with its bristly, brush-cut stand of hair in time to the music. Sooner or later he would play *Très Moutarde.* There was a special reason for this; its tune had a nostalgic appeal to graduates of Pittsburgh's Peabody High School, some of whom were always present. Five Peabodians, high-school friends, had reassembled in New York City in the late teens — after varying college careers and varying experiences in World War One. They were Malcolm Cowley (Harvard and a volunteer as an ambulance driver in France); Kenneth Burke; James Light; Mary Blair (Carnegie Tech School of the Theatre, later a leading actress with the Provincetown Players and the first wife of Edmund Wilson); and I (Ohio State University and some work in war-connected industry). Kenneth, Malcolm, Jimmie and I had all been editors of or contributors to Peabody's literary monthly, *The Peabody*. We were also sports-minded — loyal rooters for Peabody's champion football team. A football song, played by the band and sung by the rooters at 1913 and 1914 games, had been set to the tune of *Très Moutarde*: "Peabody excels by far — Each player is a star — Fast as a motor car —" Hart was delighted to play it, to please Malcolm and me and other Peabodians at our Squarcialupi evenings.

On the New Year's Eve of 1925 John Squarcialupi assigned our crowd a special room for our celebration. A few days later Hart reported, in a letter to his mother: "Our party at Squarcialupi's (what a name!) was a delight! I was sent out to get some more victrola needles about midnight, and before I got back the whistles began to blow. . . . People began throwing their arms around each other, dancing and singing. Whereat I went into such an ecstasy as only that moment of all the year affords me. I hugged my companion and started singing Gregorian chants or something of my own version approaching them, and I hope in good Latin. O New York is the place to celebrate New Year's! There is such spirit in everyone, such cordiality!" Later he planned as a section of *The Bridge* — but never wrote — a long poem to be called "New Year's Whistles."

Our dining circle was broken up in June of 1925, but only to reconvene seventy miles away in Pawling, New York. Within the preceding year I had divorced Jimmie Light, married Bill Brown, given up my job at *Telling*

Tales (leaving Allen Tate in charge), and moved to the country. This last sentence is accurate but not illuminating. Looking back, I wonder how I could have done all I did during that interim and still have enjoyed life as I was doing. Youth; is that the answer? Health and strength seem more likely. Hannah Josephson recently said to me: "Susie, I recall you as always 'singing' in those days. You made me and others want to 'sing.' When you appeared, I felt gay and happy." I'm Welsh — and the Welsh love to sing, even when they have no voice for it, like me. Hart, a non-singer, was a constant prodder of me to "sing" just as I prodded him to "tickle" the keys of a piano. I'll compress, instead of illuminating, my practical doings: an exacting, responsible full-time job; frequent conferences with my divorce lawyer in Bridgeport, bringing my chief witnesses at least once; shopping, cooking for frequent guests, keeping my flat, my clothes and *me* clean — no easy job; renting a room in Cos Cob, Connecticut, from friends of Fitzi, from which I could commute to my job and meet my divorce appointments; driving to my divorce hearing through a dreadful storm in Romolo's Stutz Bearcat, with loyal Blanche Hays as my star witness. Eventually I received a decree, calling for a period of delay before remarriage. At last plans could be made.

Notables and near-notables were involved in my divorce. Bill's plan, and mine, was to have an inconspicuous civil marriage. His plan, and mine, was to move to the country as soon as possible. We had at last found the right place, right near Fitzi's, after looking far afield. I was ready to give up Jones Street at last; we each had arranged for work we could do in the country. Everybody I knew envied me my Jones Street flat; I turned it over to Jimmie Light, who was also planning re-marriage. I left the furniture intact, but I took my phonograph records and I expected my choice of the books, a few of which had filtered down from our marriage years. I didn't get it; we came near having our first real quarrel over the books. Jimmie and his second wife lived at Jones Street for a year or so. This marriage ended only with his death, a few years ago. We always kept in close touch. His wife Patti told me that some of his last words, dying, were: "Get Susie — get Susie." We had, I think, become brother and sister. Our families lived near each other in Pittsburgh. Jimmie was several years older than I, and of English birth. He had first seen me as a "little girl"; he had not sought me out until he recognized me as a "brilliant" student at Peabody High School. I think he wanted to "shape" me, as his creation. We were better off as good friends.

Bill and I had bought an isolated, unmodernized, pre-Revolution farmhouse, with about one hundred acres and surrounded by ancient, gnarled apple orchards, right on the Connecticut line and near the house of Eleanor Fitzgerald in Sherman, Connecticut. We had found our spot while spending weekends with Fitzi. Hart resigned his job at Sweet's and joined us at "Robber Rocks," as we called it. He shared our labors on the house, his special task being to paint the weathered, dried-out clapboards a gleaming white. Late in July his mother summoned him to Cleveland to help dismantle the Crane house on 115th Street, which she had just sold. It was from there that his next letter was written.

Letter #3. To WSB and SJB. From 1709 East 115th Street, Cleveland. August 3, 1925

Dear Robbers:

This morning makes it one week that I have survived the turmoil. At least half of what we had intended to sell has been carted off and breathing is becoming somewhat easier. Even so, the family is saving enough to make the use of the fire escape necessary when they betake themselves to an apartment next spring. Minds are changed each day about what I am to have preserved for myself — so much so that I at times feel enough indifference to make any surrenders. But I'll probably ship my desk along to your Rocks and certainly several cases of books, assorted atrocities, but interesting to the rural minded. One, history of the Danes, which I was surprised to find among grandfather's books, may clear up certain enigmas, etc. And there is the darling little unreliable Everyman's Encyclopedia for future references. There may also be some pillows and bedding.

It does pay to travel, though. I am being translated into Hungarian, or whatever "their" language is called. Some friend of the Rychtariks — two years here — formerly of the MA group in Vienna and a perfect jumping-jack for intensity. In turn I am invited to reword into proper paraphrases his rather hobbling translations of his own poems, at which I am rather embarrassed. Cannibal songs and Adam before the Cross, etc. — such titles and subjects. Mad about Whitman as all those young continentals seem to be.

In spite of the hurly-burly here I can't help conjecturing the programs and celebrations at Robber Rocks. Dear Dorcas is still moist, I hope, and Charlie still generous! I have a nostalgia for the road leading past the — or it should be: "ye olde Tate place." All of which means that I still intend to get back as soon as possible.

Allen — It was good news to hear about the *Guardian* and damned pleasant to hear from you at all. You must let me know how Caroline is "doing," as Grandma says, and where you are moving as soon as decided. With love — Hart

The setting. — Dear Robbers or Banditti, Tories or Torarians were Hart's usual greetings for Bill and me, from the various names local oldtimers gave to our spot in the woods, also to a nearby historic cave, which during the Revolutionary War was used as a refuge by a band that preyed on the two-wheeled carts supplying Washington's Army encamped in the area. This cave was called either Robber Rocks or Tory Cave, depending upon the speaker's political coloration. The carts moved along the long-since-abandoned Coldspring Turnpike on which our house had been built before 1776. Hart was much taken both with the name Robber Rocks and with its alternate Tory Hill, as he was with the place itself. He wrote ecstatic letters to his mother about his life there. Our life there *was* good.

"Dear Dorcas" was a cow owned by Charlie Jennings, the farmer from whom we bought our house, his boyhood home. By our time he and his wife Hattie lived in a much grander house a mile away, now owned by Henry Allen Moe, long the dispenser of Guggenheim Foundation grants. — Charlie's "generosity": he had his own cider mill; his cellar was always filled with casks of his good hard cider, as ours was to be the following fall and winter. Charlie served the cider, to men only, in the cellar, never in the house which was Hattie's domain. Hart and Bill were frequent cellar guests. On one red-letter occasion Charlie took me down into its cool depths to give me a ladylike sip of his cherry wine.

"Ye olde Tate place": Charlie had told us of a good buy on our road, a small house in good shape which a local housepainter had acquired for payment of taxes, about $100, and which, Charlie thought, he might sell for $500. While visiting us over the Fourth of July in 1925, Allen and Caroline Tate wistfully looked it over, though, as Caroline said, "We couldn't buy an extra Woolworth dinner plate."

The "Guardian": Allen had written to Hart that he had arranged for the publication in *The Guardian* of four of Hart's "Voyages," to be introduced by Allen's essay on Hart's poetry. See *Letter #6* for the outcome.

Letter #4. To WSB and SJB. From Cleveland. Mid-
          August, 1925.
Dear Bill and Sue:

I only hope I shall be able to get away with another Indian rug. The last was a pretty clean haul, nobody having missed the article even yet, which is possibly an improvement even on my biscuit snatching at Sherman's central emporium. But there is so much hysteria around here that I doubt it would be noticed much if the house slid en masse for fifty feet. A word from you is a brace to the nerves; even though I can't get an uninterrupted five minutes to answer I hope you'll keep it up. Meanwhile you must begin plans for an extension to your house to accommodate the Crane antiquities, portraits, libraries and knick-knacks from Halifax. Nothing will be shipped until about the 4th of September and then it will be sent freight (to Patterson). So even though I don't arrive until the third week in September I'll be there when it arrives. I should like to be back at Tory Hill within a week, but I've been over-ruled emphatically, and inasmuch as my carfare hangs in the balance I'll have to remain throughout the first ten days or so in next month.

Last Saturday afternoon I broke away and called on Bill Sommer at his country place between here and Akron. I was almost made to feel as I have on Tory Hill. The country about his place ("Brandywine") is so similar to yours. The little white schoolhouse studio he works in was filled with some marvelous fresh work, and I've been presented with two drawings that will make you blink.

It is interesting to find that you have been to see Matty: I was particularly thinking about him the very days that you were there. I hope his jeopardies have been removed. . . .

I cannot resist longer in describing my torments from my week of debauchery (wine-bibbing only) (O yes, there was one pleasant occasion) — enroute through New York. I'm just getting over it, and am still on the strictest diet. It has led to a final resolution to hop the water wagon until my next birthday, at which time I shall bound down with a crash — but not until then! What is life without a bladder! But when I think of poor Malcolm (Allen wrote me about it, too) I realize that ALL is folly, and one might as well have as good and unrighteous a time as not! What a persistent capacity for physical accidents that good poet, critic and friend seems to have! I've been wondering what happened after that to Little Eva.

Here come some aunts and cousins so I'll have to close my ditty box and blow out smoke lamp —

hart

The setting. — The "Indian rug" had arrived by mail, un-announced, the first wave of the Cleveland deluge that was to follow.

"Bill Sommer" was the Ohio painter to whom Hart dedicated his poem "Sunday Morning Apples," which was published in *White Buildings.* Hart tried several times to ar-range for the exhibition of Sommer's paintings in New York, without much cooperation from the painter. Later on, Hart discovered that Sommer had little interest in selling; he couldn't bear to part with his paintings except as gifts to friends, preferring to earn his living in a lithographing plant.

Bill and I had driven down to Katonah in Westchester, to spend a day with the Matty Josephsons. Matty had quit his Wall Street job and retired to Katonah with his wife Hannah and their baby Eric. His "jeopardies" was a threat-ened mastoidectomy. The Josephsons soon abandoned Ka-tonah and settled in our much wilder country.

Hart's "wine bibbing" was to celebrate his twenty-sixth birthday. Of course, his "water wagon" did not last until July 21, 1926, but it did persist during his stay at Robber Rocks in September, a very pleasant period for all of us.

Malcolm's "physical accidents" refers, in this case, to a broken arm caused by cranking his Model-T Ford, called Little Eva, while enroute from Staten Island, where he and Peggy lived that summer, to his family's farm in Belsano, Pennsylvania.

Letter #5. To WSB. From Wade Park Manor, Cleve-
             land. August 27, 1925
Dear Bill:

The above address will be good until I leave — prob-ably about ten days from now. This ought to bring me back to you in about a fortnight — with two or three days in NY on the way. I shall very possibly be one of the elite to witness the Tate ceremonies, but unless I get away from here pretty soon I shall be but an insane godfather for any child to be doomed by, and my hair will be white enough to play King Lear.

The following bundles left here yesterday for Patterson, N.Y., addressed directly to Slater Brown and freight prepaid: 5 cases of books; 1 trunk (filled with blankets, china, pictures, etc.); 1 desk; 1 chair. Five separate pieces in all. They may possibly arrive before I get there (the schedule for freight is uncertain) but I suggest that you let me share the burden of transportation from Patterson to Robber Rocks and wait until I arrive. (I'm not referring to trucking costs, which are, of course, my obligation anyway — but rather to arrangements, lifting, etc.) Do, please, acknowledge receipt of notice from station master, however, if he writes you. . . . And forgive me if my directions sound like Old Mother Bunch of Dubuque. Believe me, I'm in a strange state.

Yours for the Rocks in September (at least by the 15th) — and my love to Sue.

as ever

HART

The setting. — The Tates were expecting a baby (hence Hart's earlier inquiry as to how Caroline was "doing") and had asked Hart to be on hand as godfather, if he could make it. But he was back at Robber Rocks before the event.

The "bundles" from Cleveland: We didn't have to put on an addition to "accommodate the Crane knick-knacks from Halifax" but we did have to clear out our largest downstairs room, which became Hart's Room. His desk and chair were installed there. Bill and Hart made rough bookshelves to hold the "darling little unreliable Everyman's Encyclopedia" and a host of other books. The antiquities were scattered about, pictures hung, the Navajo rug laid on the floor of wide pine boards. We lent his room a Currier and Ives print that came with the house: a colored lithograph, headed "Barnum's Gallery of Wonders," portraying "Miss Jane Campbell, the Great Connecticut Giantess. 18 years old, weighs 628 pounds. To be seen at BAR-NUM'S MUSEUM at all hours, every day and evening." Charlie Jennings had told us, diffidently and therefore credibly, that Miss Campbell had been a friend of his mother, Rosella Jennings, who had lived in our house until her death a year or so before at the age of eighty-seven. Hart had fallen in love with Jane at first sight. She still hangs at Robber Rocks, in her elegant dark-blue satin evening dress, every one of her 628 pounds exuding comfortable good-humor.

Among the "etc." items in the trunk was a delightful jumble of female garments, what Caroline Tate called "Hart's maternal finery." These Hart distributed among his women friends. My chief prize was a pair of black-and-white-check riding breeches. Fitzi received a good topcoat, brown hound's-tooth, the sight of which, on Fitzi, Hart always enjoyed, even in its final stage as a gardening coat. Caroline was awarded a baby-blue negligee. A young girl's lace dress, white, well-beribboned in pale pink, has been used by several generations for charades.

The Everyman's Encyclopedia came to a sad end during the winter of 1926–1927, when Candlewood Lake was created by flooding some six thousand acres of farm land, thereby evicting untold numbers of rats that had lived cozily in hundreds of barns. The rats invaded all the buildings within a few miles of the new lake, including Robber Rocks, which we had closed up for the winter on leaving for work in New York. When we made our first early-spring visit, we found all the volumes of the encyclopedia in a desolate mixed-up mass on the floor. The rats had devoured the glue that held them together.

The Navajo rug has had a better fate; since 1966 it has been on the floor of Malcolm Cowley's study in Sherman, Connecticut. It got off to a bad start, because of Hart's cleanliness bug. Before laying it on the floor of our West Room, Hart induced me to help him wash it in our tin washtub. As I had feared, the colors (red, brown, and white) ran somewhat under our crude handling, but Hart pronounced this an improvement. Very heavy when wet, it broke our clothesline when we threw it over, coming down on both of us and knocking us off our feet. When Hart gave up his rooms at Addie Turner's in 1930, his desk, chair, and rug were sheltered at Fitzi's for a time and then came back to Robber Rocks, their first home in the East. The rug still shows signs of its amateur shampoo, the reason for which was that Hart had no money for dry-cleaning. We were all living to a large extent on our vegetable garden and apple orchard, on wild berries and grapes, on quince jam, supplemented inexpensively with Charlie's bacon, milk, and eggs, hoe cakes made of "water ground" white cornmeal imported by mail from the Pawmunkey Mills in Kentucky — or was it Virginia? — the latter a Tate influence. Bill was earning some translation money while working on a novel. I received $10 each for explanations of "Famous American Slogans" from my old magazine, such as "Fifty-four Forty or Fight," "Tippecanoe and Tyler, Too." Hart alone had no income for the time being. Dry-cleaning was out of the question.

Letter #6.   To WSB and SBJ. From 110 Columbia Heights, Brooklyn.   October 21, 1925

Dear Tories:

There have been numerous "celebrations" besides the already recounted one (by Bina) on the great transaction, and the Punch Palazzo has had due patronage. The engrossing female at most of these has been "Rideshalk-Godding," as I have come to call her, and thus far the earnest ghost of acidosis has been kept well hence. My real regret, however, is that I just missed getting the pick of jobs of the S. Am. line, last steamer — said occupation being deck yeoman at 20 minutes work a day, all freedom of ship, mess with officers or any first class passengers that seemed colloquial, white uniform, brass buttons, cap; meditation on the sun deck all day long, and seventy-five dollars a month clear sailing! The chief officer had already approved me, but before I could get over to the offices for final approbation they had already sent someone else over to the ship. We must have passed under the river. However, I noticed that my questionnaire (filed last June) had won an OK sign in the upper right corner, and I have been told to come around again on the 26th when the next boat arrives. I'm not waiting for that, however, as I need instant cash and there is not one chance in a hundred of a similar vacancy soon. Otherwise I have finished the "Wine Menagerie" and have sent it off, along with "Passage," to *The Criterion*. Since the last (yesterday) *Guardian* has come out *without* the "Voyages." I am thinking of trying to become a literary ex-patriot. It's just as tiresome as ever. This issue contains a lot of tommy-rot by Seaver and an "announcement" into the bargain that reads unforgivably: — "Voyages, four remarkable poems by Allen Tate" . . . will appear in the next issue!

Emil took me to see "Arms and the Man" last night, and I found it very amusing, if ancient. Have not seen Chaplin yet. Broadway is, to me, a depressing promenade, and unless someone urges me thither I don't seem to trickle up there. Have you heard about the death of Matty's father? (I don't know why I crowd so many divergencies into one paragraph.) Elbano is here at 110 packing up his ditty boxes, etc., to go to St. Louis today. I have had a room to sleep in at 65 Columbia Heights as the Opffer Bros. have kept this joint well filled, but this is still my address, and I expect to re-install myself very soon.

Am on my way up to *The Dial* to have lunch with K.B. and shall try to bag a review or briefers from the Rt. Rev. Miss Mountjoy. A momentous morning: Frank is going to try to corner Liveright on my vol. also.

Mrs. Boving tells me you have been pressing apples, grapes and everything in sight. I wish I could be with you. The city certainly isn't pleasant for long. Meanwhile I hope for money and good luck before June. Love — Hart

The setting. — After his September at Robber Rocks, Hart had gone job-hunting in New York, while Bill and I harvested our crops, tame and wild, and prepared in other ways to settle in for the winter in our unheated (except by wood stoves), isolated farmhouse.

The "great transaction" refers to Hart's efforts to buy ten or so acres from Bina Flynn, who with her husband-to-be, Romolo, had just bought a nearby farmhouse with generous acreage, a larger, also pre-Revolutionary, mate to our house.

In our early months at Robber Rocks, Bill and I had been infected with "convert's fever"; we propagandized our close friends to buy land and a house near us. Johanne and Henrik Boving, older friends with cash in the bank, were the first buyers, soon to be followed by Bina and Romolo. Eventual settlers were Malcolm and Peggy Cowley, Matthew and Hannah Josephson, Robert and Elsa Coates, Peter and Ebie Blume. The Tates were the first to be infected, as Hart's mention of Ye Olde Tate Place shows. Other prospective Tate sites followed, but circumstances were not propitious. Hart, too, was set on acquiring his own "place," and at first Bill and I helped him in his search. We came near settling him on an isolated eighty-acre abandoned farm overgrown with sumac and poison ivy, with only a foundation in lieu of a house, a mile from a public road. I had forgotten the zeal Bill and I put into our land search for Hart until recently, when I came across a letter that I had written to Hart on September 4, 1925, just before he left the "turmoil" of Cleveland to return to Robber Rocks. This letter has landed in the Hart Crane Collection at Columbia University; my guess is that it was found among his mother's papers on her death in 1947, and was sold, or given, to Columbia. A strange experience, unexpectedly coming across one's own old forgotten unimportant words in a great library. The letter reads:

Dear Hart: — I'm glad you're coming soon. Here's an item you may wish to know before you leave Cleveland: Jennings offers to lend you two hundred dollars to buy that 80 acre place, if you can raise the other two hundred. He'll take a three-year mortgage on it, and he thinks you can easily make quite a bit on selling the place, if you find it impossible to build any sort of house. I do hope you can manage this. It really is such a good opportunity that I'd hate to see you miss it, even from a business standpoint. If you couldn't manage anything else during the next four or five years, you and Bill could construct some sort of cabin on it. We have gone over the whole place and there are several fine sites on it, and enough trees to make a log cabin, if you wished — certainly enough stones to build a stone house. If you can't get the money outright, perhaps you could buy it for your mother or grandmother. In this case they would be absolutely protected against loss. I doubt if another such opportunity will ever be found in this section of the country. The Bovings have bought the green house opposite us: perhaps I have already told you this. Bill is very anxious to have you get this place. Jennings has taken a great shine to you, apparently. He told us that this year he would press cider only for himself, us and you!

Bina is due to make a week end visit soon. When you are in N.Y. it might be wise for you to phone her. If you happen to be coming up on a Friday, you could travel together.

Love,

Sue

To the naked eye, Jennings looked perfectly sober, and the offer was made in the presence of Bill, me, and his wife.

Fortunately for Hart, and for our good conscience, the sale met with obstacles. Bill and I soon recovered from the fever and realized how impractical such a move would be for a lone man with no aptitude for the manual skills called for by primitive country living. The very letter in which he exults in the "great transaction" also recounts his desire to be footloose and on the move. So, when Hart switched his aim to buying land from Bina — again with no house and poor access to a public road — we all went along with him only because dissuasion obviously upset him. Didn't we want him to settle down as a neighbor?, his attitude implied. He borrowed $200 from his Cleveland friends, Richard and Charlotte Rychtarik, and Bina accepted it, mainly to save it for him. The "great transaction" never reached the deed stage, and Bina returned the money.

"Rideshalk-Godding" was Laura Riding, the poet, then Mrs. Laura Riding Gottschalk, a member of the Nashville "Fugitive" group of poets that also included Allen Tate. Shortly after this letter, Hart brought Laura to Robber Rocks — they were driven up by the Bobbas — and a tempestuous week-end ensued. Hart and Laura cascaded into and out of most of the households in our small literary community, Hart carrying with him a jug of hard cider, playing jazz records, dancing, shouting their literary opinions, picking up a driver here and there to chauffeur them to the next stop, leaving each household somewhat the worse for wear but with echoes of merriment in the air. Robber Rocks — the starting and ending point — bore the brunt but survived in serenity. As soon as Hart heard it, he abandoned his "Rideshalk-Godding" for an older more descriptive phrase: "Laura Riding Roughshod." He found it more entertaining, as, it seemed, did Laura, for they remained friends. Laura later shifted her scene of operations to England, where Hart spent Christmas in 1928, with her and Robert Graves in the Graves' houseboat on the Thames.

The job as "deck yeoman": Hart made several attempts to get some such job at sea, as a way to avoid an enervating advertising copy-writer's job and to "see the world" at the same time. He failed.

The *Guardian:* This reports the misfiring of Allen Tate's efforts to advance Hart's poetic reputation, mentioned in *Letter #3.*

Then came another event, affecting Allen's life rather than Hart's, at the time, though it had a later effect on Hart's: Allen lost his job at *Telling Tales.* He had committed the indiscretion of correcting the grammar in an office memo from the boss. So the Tates decided to give up a too expensive New York apartment and live inexpensively in the country for the winter. They rented the major portion of Addie Turner's large old house at the crossroads one-half mile from Robber Rocks, fully furnished, for $10 a month. They moved in on a miserable, rainy November day, with Bill driving them from the station in our $35 Model T, barely able to make it through the muddy, rutted dirt road.

With Allen's leaving, *Telling Tales* disappears from these pages. To cover this phase as it touched on Hart's life we must go back to an earlier date, when Allen and I had escaped scot-free from a worse boner than correcting the boss's grammar, if such there be. One of my jobs was to divide into appropriate episodes the novels we published serially and to write a "teaser" for the next instalment. On one occasion either haste or Freud had induced me to write: "Do not fail to miss the next instalment of this thrilling . . ." etc. Allen passed it by in his proofreading, and it appeared in the magazine. But nobody noticed it, except, eventually, me, in horror. Hart gleefully picked up the phrase, using it when denouncing a piece of writing he disliked: "Do not fail to miss this disgusting, nauseating" — but I am unable to recall the originals nor can I invent equivalents to Hart's vigorous invectives.

My office on East Eleventh Street near University Place was a convenient rendezvous at five o'clock. Hart came by frequently, hoping to lure Allen or Bina or me for an after-work drink at the Poncino Palazzo, or Punchino Palace, as we called it, a grim six-by-eight hole behind a delicatessen on West Fourth Street, where for fifteen or twenty cents we drank lethal speakeasy "rum" in hot water, made almost potable by a twist of lemon peel. Often Hart hoped to be invited home to dinner by one of us; his hope was realized more often than not. With the sanction of a complaisant boss, Bill Clayton, the *Telling Tales* office, after office hours, was used as the editorial and mailing center for the booklet *Aesthete 1925,* a lively reply to the Anglo-Irish critic Ernest Boyd's satire "Aesthete Model 1924," in the first issue of

H. L. Mencken's *American Mercury*. From five to nine in the evenings for a week in February the T.T. office was buzzing with Malcolm Cowley, Matty Josephson, Kenneth Burke, Bill Brown, Hart, and Peggy Baird, who did the illustrations. Bill's contribution to *Aesthete 1925* was a "Chanson" signed by the name of the fictitious editor Walter S. Hankel. Before it got into print, "Chanson" bore a few traces of other hands. In it Bill took a friendly poke at Gorham Munson's occasional lapses into a pompous style:

CHANSON
"I"
    said Mr. M as we crossed the street together
"am compelled to reject this
    poem ..."
    At that moment a terrific detonation interrupted his
    dictum
    and Mr. M soared into space astride
    the lid of a
    man-hole

    The last I saw of him he was miles high
    trying to climb off
    In suchwise did Mr. M ride into Heaven.
    Hallelujah!

Gorham Munson had published a review of T. S. Eliot's *The Waste Land* in the first issue of *1924* (July, 1924) in which he had written: "I am compelled to reject the poem as a sustained harmoniously functioning structural unit."

In later years, a misconception arose that Hart Crane had written "Chanson." Was this attribution first published in *Transition?* — I can't remember now. Then Brom Weber found "Hart Crane" written across "Chanson" in the copy of *Aesthete 1925* among Allen Tate's papers in the Princeton Library and made this attribution in his biography of Crane. Even Matthew Josephson, an active collaborator on *Aesthete 1925,* picked up this mistaken attribution, and so noted the authorship in his *Life among the Surrealistes* (1965). One can understand how this came about, because the numerous collaborators freely used the signature of the fictitious editor, not always knowing who had written what. Hart Crane did not write "Chanson."

Both Boyd's "Aesthete Model 1924" and *Aesthete 1925* were meant to be humorous. The young compilers of the latter prefixed this "Guarantee": "Every article contained in this issue of A. '25 is guaranteed to be in strictly bad taste." Perhaps they succeeded beyond their fondest hope, for humor is likely to be evanescent. In the Twenties "good taste" as a shibboleth to belabor was on a par with the current use of "The Establishment" and "The Power Structure." A quality in *Aesthete 1925* that was not volatile is in the late Charles Sheeler's black-and-white drawing used as the cover, the original of which hung in Hart's room at Robber Rocks. It now hangs in mine.

At the time of the Aesthetes '24 and '25 I was leading a mildly double life. Through my connection with the Provincetown Players I was also associating with a theatrical circle centering on the Theatre Guild's personnel, at whose gatherings Ernest Boyd occasionally appeared, his wife being a play agent. I ran into Boyd at one of these gatherings at Lee Simonson's. Boyd seized upon me and clamored to be put in touch immediately, by telephone, with the Aesthetes '25. "I don't even know them!" he wailed. "I wouldn't recognize them on the street!" So I gave him Matty's number on King Street, where several of the Aesthetes '25 were likely to be. I heard him say: "This is — oh-ah — Ernest Boyd. Oh-ah — Hart Crane? Would you mind telling me where your poems appear?" I could hear Hart's resonant Midwest voice crackling on, and Boyd relayed Hart's reply to me as: "Oh-ah — Ernest Boyd? My poems appear behind pianos and up chimneys. Would you mind telling me where *your* poems appear?"

This is far away from *Letter #6,* yet before going on to *Letter #7* and Dutchess County, we must wander farther, through a long aside on the "Opffer Bros." referred to in

Paragraph 2, for this reference evokes a need to describe Hart's life at 110 Columbia Heights in Brooklyn. Emil and the late Elbano, a marine engineer, were the sons of Emil Opffer, Sr., the owner-editor of the New York Danish weekly *Nordlyset,* and of Mrs. Johanne (Opffer) Boving, then married to Henrik Boving, a research scientist in the Bell Telephone Laboratories. In the early Twenties Johanne had informally adopted me as a daughter, and I made my home with her during Jimmie's long absences touring Europe or the hinterland with plays. Emil regarded me as a sister. When Hart joined our social circle in 1923 he soon met Emil and became attached to him, as indeed were, and are, all my friends. Emil's exuberance excited high spirits in others — a "party" spirit. Gregarious and open-handed, he would appear unexpectedly at one's door loaded down with large bags containing Scandinavian delicacies, bottles of wine protruding, and proceed to lay out a Danish smørgasbord for all present. If the guests exceeded his supplies, he would dash out to raid his mother's larder, not far away, often returning with her to take part in his on-shore celebration. Emil was, at first, earning his living at sea as a steward; then came a year or so of editing and publishing *Nordlyset* after his father's death, and then another year as the White House correspondent for a chain of Midwest Danish newspapers. After that he became a purser on transatlantic and other routes, much in demand by skippers because of his geniality, quick wits, and general versatility. Emil is a veteran of artillery service in World War I; his hearing was permanently and seriously damaged by artillery bombardments, though this was not discovered until he was unable to qualify for the final test as a naval radio-operator, his chosen profession after demobilization.

Over the years Emil helped Hart in many ways: with cash and good cheer during depressions; and, most important to Hart, guiding him to the room at Columbia Heights overlooking Brooklyn Bridge and the Manhattan skyline, where Emil's father was living when Hart first went there, and where various members of the footloose Opffer family had lived from time to time. Recognizing their prior claims, Hart had yielded his room to the "Opffer Bros." with Emil on shore between trips and Elbano, the marine engineer, in New York between jobs, to pack up his "ditty boxes," a favorite term of Hart's which he had come across in an antiquated seaman's manual. Many suppose that Emil was an "inspiration" for Hart's "Voyages." "Voyages I" was written and published before Hart met him, with the title "Poster."

Hart did indeed "romanticize" Emil, whose ready warmth and kindness moved Hart deeply, since he needed them so much. Later on, finding that this warmth was a general rather than a particular response, he had a short period of intense disappointment during which he was a trial to a few close friends. Aided by Emil's continued evidences of friendship, such as that mentioned in this letter, he soon recovered and settled into a normal, calmer friendship on the infrequent occasions when they could meet, with Emil's regular abode being the sea and Hart wandering from place to place. Emil, now retired, lives with his wife in Munich; but they are frequently on the go, to Spain, to Italy, to his native Denmark, from which spots he has kept up over the years his practice of sprinkling his dozens, if not hundreds, of friends with picture postcards all of which are signed: "Love and kisses! Emil." His joke is that his happy marriage came about because one of his addressees took his greeting seriously.

Hart loved his room at 110 Columbia Heights, and treated it with great care, as, indeed, he did his pleasant rooms at Addie Turner's, his country home as Columbia Heights was his city home. He had a gift for order and attractive arrangement of furniture, pictures, colors. This room was not the scene of drunken riots with sailors. "Old Man Opffer" lived down the corridor from him, and Hart was set on keeping his good opinion, as an influential old-inhabitant. The "Opffer Bros." singly or together came occasionally either to Hart's room or to their father's. Emil's regular home, when in New York, was at his mother's house on West Twelfth Street, until he sublet half of Fitzi's large apartment. For a short time Hart had a room in a nearby rooming house for transients; what went on there I do not know.

I knew 110 Columbia Heights well, having been an occasional visitor there for years preceding Hart's occupancy, through my friendship with the Opffer-Boving family. Emil and I would go there to join his father before dinner, either at an Armenian restaurant on nearby Atlantic Avenue, or by taking a subway trip back to Bedford Street in Manhattan, to Passerini's where Mr. Opffer, Sr., dined regularly, holding court among an assemblage of Scandinavian expatriates, for Mr. Opffer had been the prominent owner-editor of a chain of popular newspapers in Denmark. I was introduced as a "well-known editor" on the score of my job at *Telling Tales*. After dinner we sometimes went on to a play or the opera on *Nordlyset* tickets; Emil wrote reviews for his father's paper when on shore. *Arms and the Man,* to which he took Hart, was one of these.

The three brick dwellings at 106-108-110 Columbia Heights were torn down to make way for the "Esplanade" along the Brooklyn waterfront. They had been owned by a prominent painter and art teacher, Hamilton Easter Field, the scion of an old Brooklyn Heights family, who had been born in one of them. In 1924, his adopted son, the sculptor Robert Laurent, inherited them. Field had turned his three houses into an art school and "art colony." The three buildings had been connected on the parlor and basement floors by breaking through walls and installing doors. The basements were the art school's headquarters, the three upper stories, residences, some as apartments for family living, others as single rooms. Products of the art school were scattered through lobbies and halls. There were resident painters–art teachers and their families living there, with wives and children and a scattering of writers, one of whom was John Dos Passos. The tone was that of the "arty" middle-class, those who wished to lead a quiet life in non-garish, non-modern, but also non-Greenwich-village surroundings. Hart was even able to play his phonograph in the evenings without disturbing his neighbors because of the thickness of the old walls. He was careful to keep the volume down.

Letter #7.   To MC.   From Mrs. Turner's at Pawling,
             New York.   January 3, 1926
Dear Malcolm:

The poem has been read with approval — is flatteringly apocalyptic and has the proper nautical slant.... Seriously, though, it seems to stand on its own feet as a poem and I appreciate a very great deal the tonality and direction of it in its more intimate aspects. You and Peggy have been more than good in remembering me — thanks for the photo, too.

Allen probably gave you enough of a picture of our daily operations and dissipations out here. In point of fact, I'm just beginning to get down to work — after a cyclone of mail ordering, food choring, etc. etc. We have to be provided, of course, against severe snow and a siege of weather — though there may be the mildest of days ahead.

Are you reviewing Doc. Transit anywhere? Schneider finally sent me out a copy. It intrigued me more than any such tour de force since Poe, though it has its obvious weaknesses. Some chapters, however, of great imagination. I didn't anticipate half so much from the earlier things I've read by Schneider.

I'm coming to town probably about two weeks from now, and should like to know what day or days about that period you'll be there also. You know what the Gov. of North Carolina said to the Governor of S. Carolina — ! I'm such a rum scallion that I never even planned to stay put anywhere very long in the woods. Let me hear from you soon. Allen will probably write you about the outcome of his interview (along with Wilson) with the Adelphi Press. It looks as though we'd all be published next fall.

My love to you both — Hart

Comment: Since the middle of December Hart had been living with the Tates in Mrs. Turner's house in Pawling in Dutchess County, New York. The Tates had come to live there in November, and by the time of Hart's arrival in December, the Brown and Tate families were settled in for the winter. We enjoyed our country life, even though we were snowed in for months, and the flivver was useless. For long stretches we got our milk, butter, and eggs from the Jennings on skis and snowshoes; our stores in the cellar supplied the rest. But we did not lack company. Both the Tates and the Browns had frequent house guests, who often arrived from Pawling station on a wagon sled, driven by our versatile neighbor Eva Parker, and pulled by her horse named June-oh! in recognition of his sex and the month of his birth. "Not 'Juno,' " Eva reminded us firmly, if we forgot. "Not that goddess!" Fitzi and her guests, the Bovings and theirs, also the Flynn-Bobbas, managed to get up occasionally. And from December on, there was Hart at Mrs. Turner's, enough to assure a lively social life especially at the Christmas reunion when the Cowleys and the Josephsons joined us.

Hart had survived the fall by using the Rychtariks' loan meant to buy land, through the sale of a few poems and a little aid from his father and friends. At last, reluctantly, he had appealed to the banker–art patron Otto Kahn for a loan to enable him to continue work on his long poem *The Bridge*. By December 9, Kahn had promised him $2000 and given him $1000. In tremendously high spirits, Hart joined the Tates. He was assigned two large rooms on the second floor, above the Tates' spacious suite. They were to eat together in the large kitchen, dominated by the old-fashioned wood-range used both for cooking and for heating. The adjoining pump-room was used in common by all occupants. Mrs. Turner, then along in her sixties, and her ancient stone-deaf Aunt Julia Agard, in her eighties, each had separate wings. Addie referred to each section as a "part": "my part, my aunt's part, the Tates' part, Mr. Crane's part." For the Christmas holidays, the Cowleys, up from Staten Island, were housed in "Mr. Crane's part." The Josephsons were at Robber Rocks, where a get-together was held one evening for all our friends in the Valley.

On this occasion — at Malcolm's suggestion, as I recall — Hart read his "Voyages II." The poem had been written before he left his job at *Sweet's Architectural Catalogue*. He had made a change in the last line and asked for reactions. The line had read: "The seal's findrinny gaze toward paradise." Somebody had questioned the existence of the word "findrinny." Hart had paged through both of Sweet's unabridged dictionaries, but could not find it. Neither could he recall where he had come across it, though he was confidant that he had not made it up. A respecter of dictionaries, he had decided to change the line to "The seal's wide spindrift gaze toward paradise." Some of those present advocated retaining "findrinny" for its sound and suggestibility, but this did not satisfy Hart. After the poem was published in its revised form, the following summer, Bill Brown came across "findrinny" somewhere in Melville, used in the sense Hart had intended. Malcolm Cowley has reported this incident accurately in *Exile's Return* (1937, 1951). He was misquoted in a subsequent study of Hart's life and works, in which the point was lost.

In *Letter #7* "The poem" refers to Malcolm's "The Flower in the Sea," which he had mailed to Hart on returning home after Christmas. In the 1929 edition of *Blue Juniata* it is dedicated to HHC (Harold Hart Crane), which was changed to "For Hart Crane" in the enlarged edition of 1968. The poem is *about* Hart; he is imagined to be speaking it, as in these lines:

> Jesus I saw, crossing Times Square
> with John the Beloved, and they bade me stop;
> my hand touched theirs.
>
> Visions from the belly of a bottle.
>
> The sea, white, white,
> the flower in the sea,

the white fire glowing in the flower;
and sea and fire and flower one,
the world is one, falsehood and truth
one, morning and midnight, flesh and vision
one.

"Doctor Transit" is the title of Isidor Schneider's first novel. And whatever the Adelphi Press plan may have been, its collapse is reported in the next letter.

Before we go on to *Letter #8* and March, another January diversion from our snowbound life occurred. This time it came from Romolo Bobba, far away in Canada where he had been marooned for months taking care of the delicate intricacies of his Italian-Canadian-American import business. Book-length telegrams began to arrive from Canada, most of them to Bina, then on her lucrative job as editor of *Ranch Romances* in my old publishing firm, and, in January, one or two came to me, relayed from the Pawling operator over Mrs. Turner's phone, with Hart as the transcriber and delivery boy. One day Hart burst in our door, excited and giggling. "Has Romolo gone *mad!*" he shouted. "Or has he taken to writing bad poetry?" From his penciled notes he read the gist of Romolo's telegram:

"Sue, Bill, imperative you come to Montreal. Have completed all arrangements. Bina reports your negative response. Phone her immediately. Bina needs both of you here. I guarantee you and Bill a glorious time. *Don't forget Sue you are America to Bina and me.*"

Hart declaimed the underlined sentence, then: "Now tell me — is that poetry, or is it madness? As to that, Sue: you're America to me. You're the Jersey mosquito flats. You're Pittsburgh, the Smoky City. You're the Midwest Breadbasket. You're — " Instead of going on to the Rocky Mountains he chanted: "Oh Susanna — you're off to Mon - tre-al-i-aye — "

In everyday language, the poetry meant that Romolo feared his precious Bina might balk at a Montreal wedding unless Bill and I were there, as participants and as chaperones for her. Long ago Romolo had proposed that we should have a "double wedding" in Canada. But Bina's Mexican divorce had been long delayed; Bill and I had gone ahead with our plans.

There were sound reasons why Romolo should be married in Canada. I do not feel it necessary to go into these in a book about Hart Crane. A few years later, the United States, like Romolo, was to become anti-Fascismo. Bina had not held us to the Canadian marriage. But there was no resisting Romolo, and we went. I was glad we did; Bina would have been in a most uncomfortable situation, among strangers, if we had not gone, so we had a double religious ceremony, grand style, as Romolo had planned, with fifty or more Montrealans, carefully selected by Romolo, as witnesses and celebrants. Then followed a banquet-style dinner, fine wines, flowery toasts from Romolo's Italian associates, and much admiration from the Scotch-British types that one finds in Montreal — those who had a sense that Bill and I came from the American educated middle class, from which they did not spring in their own circle. Call it snobbism. As Romolo had known, it was easy to impress them, just through one's speech and what one talked about. Romolo would no longer be regarded with suspicion, or hope, as a high-powered American gangster, which he wasn't. He had to get that out of his way, before he could dedicate himself to making a good life for Bina.

Hart was the first to understand this. Going back to Romolo's urgent and very Italianate telegram: as soon as Hart had had enough fun, I put on my ba-ba coat and walked back with him to Mrs. Turner's on the narrow path we had all stamped down through the snow, to phone Bina that our response was now "positive." Hart walked ahead of me. Then he burst out: "Romolo's a great guy, isn't he, Sue? He knows what he wants and what needs to be done, and then he *does* it! He loves Bina 'with every fibre of his being' — the cliché applies." Then he stopped, blocking me on the path, and looking back over his shoulder as if to make sure I was listening, said: "I wish there were more men like Romolo."

Letter #8.   To M.C.   From Pawling, New York.   March 28, 1926

Dear Malcolm:

The news of your plans for the summer is good to hear! We're all anticipating the first of May — though you *will* be a little distant. Five miles walking says Mrs. Turner, coming out of her Aunt's part with the tea.

After a perfect spasm of sentiment and "inspection" I was released from the fond embrace of my relatives in Cleveland — only to fall into rather more than less spasmodic embraces in N.Y. — a one-night spree — on my way back. Since which I have been reading the philosophies of the East until I actually dream in terms of the Vedanta scriptures. Also am finding Marco Polo pleasant to incorporate in the subconscious.

I've often wondered how you got home that night. After you left I was roused from my stupor by an amazing scandal at the next table. Benet, Wylie and some others discussing Nathalia Crane — who, it seems, doesn't write at all. Her father does the trick — works off "suppressed desires" that way, etc., etc. I was very good after that and stormed over to the Albert, lectured the clerk for not admitting my friends, and went to bed, tout seul.

The next morning after the next I was discovering that my Mother knows how to mix the best cocktails I ever drank.

Are you going ahead with the Boyd proposal? I think you should — a fine weapon against further attacks from that gent. again — and not, however, implying any concession whatever on your part.

I wish I had a lyric or so to circulate, like Allen. He suddenly sprouted last week and has been going ever since. A letter from Eliot indicates that the New Criterion may take some of his poems. The Adelphi matter has definitely fallen through.

Carolyn has gone to Washington and points south for a coupla weeks.

Wish you'd write. Best to Peggy

Hart

Comment: Hart had yielded to his "rum scallion's" desires and had enjoyed two flings in New York. From the first, in January, he returned bearing some "beautiful and rare Congo wood-carving" and an "African chieftain's shield," which we were to see in many of his masquerades. He had also commissioned a casting of Gaston Lachaise's much admired seagull. Then, in March, he had stopped at the Hotel Albert in New York for a few days, en route to Cleveland to see his ailing Grandma Hart and to encourage his mother's marriage to Charles Curtis. He had spent an evening with Malcolm, adding his pleas to ours that the Cowleys forsake Staten Island and move to our neighborhood. Charlie Jennings had found a suitable tenant house in nearby Sherman, owned by his old friend Akin Briggs.

The usually amiable critic William Rose Benét, by then married to Elinor Wylie, was a chief detractor of Hart's poetry. The "child wonder" Nathalia Crane, thirteen years old in 1926, had a tremendous vogue, which soon waned, yet she is still preserved in the 1968 edition of *Bartlett's Familiar Quotations* with two four-line jingles, one of which begins: "Oh, I'm in love with the janitor's boy/ And the janitor's boy loves me."

Letter #9. To WSB and SJB. From Nueva Gerona, Isle of Pines. May 7, 1926

Dear Sue and Bill:

It is still one day less than a week since we sailed, our second on the island. Frank got Ward Line accommodations, which cut a day off the sea; and we were rather sorry. Still, passing Pam Bitch, My ammy and other Coney Islands at midnight wasn't especially thrilling; that part of the trip was too close shore. But Havana was more and better than I had imagined. Architecture rather like Chirico — some Spanish "plasteresque" — and physically-metaphysically suggestive. But mostly on the surface; there isn't other evidence.

F's Spanish brought us off all beaten paths. We didn't visit an American haunt except the steamship office. The rest was mostly bars, cafes and theatres — filled with blacks, reds, browns, greys and every permutation and combination of southern bloods that you can imagine. Corona-Coronas, of course, for 15¢, marvelous sherry, cognac, vermouth and "Tropical" (the beer that I was talking about). Am. boats seem to be easy, by the way; we had St. Julienne and Sauterne all the way down at table. Then we went to the Alhambra, a kind of Cuban National Winter Garden Burlesque. Latin "broadness" was somewhat veiled from me as far as the dialogue went, but actions went farther than apparently even the East Side can stand.

Gratings and balconies and narrow streets with plenty of whores nodding. The day of our departure a great fleet of American destroyers landed. Streets immediately became torrents of uniforms — one sailor had exactly the Chinese mustache effect that I aspire to. But no Jack Fitzin — his boat must have passed to Brooklyn — passed in the night. Taxis anywhere in town for only 20¢, but that's about the only cheap feature. Great black bushed buxom Jamaican senoritas roared laughter at us; old women hobbled up offering lottery tickets (I finally got one on a hunch). The whole town is hyper-sensual and mad — i.e. has no apparent direction, destiny or purpose; Cummings' paradise. I shall have to go up for a real spree sometime when cash is plentiful; meanwhile this isle is enough Eden.

Poor Mrs. Simpson hadn't expected us for at least three days more — and F, of course, the extra party, almost bowled her over at first sight. She had a violent coughing fit, at which I thought the fragile frame of her would break and during which a parrot screamed from a corner some-

54

where, "Damned poor dinner!" She has recovered and is really lovable and quite the contrary of all I expected. I've had one pleasant shock after another. The house is much more spacious than I had remembered, the island much more beautiful. The approach from the sea is like the Azores, F. says. To me, the mountains, strange greens, native thatched huts, perfume, etc., brought me straight to Melville. The heat *is* different from northern summer heat and the parroty phrase does hold — "it's always cool in the shade." It was cool enough for F. to put a coat on at sundown today, "breezes prevail." Oleanders and mimosas in full bloom now make the air almost too heavy with perfume; it's another world — and a little like Rimbaud. I'm surprised that I didn't carry away more definite impressions from my first visit 11 years ago.

We discovered a beach yesterday, very near our house. We bathed late in the day and the water was almost too warm. The rest of the time we've wandered over the grove, bought fish, played with a baby owl that suddenly appeared, drunk punch, picked coconuts (which are a meal by themselves). You ought to see that owlet (Pythagoras) make away with a chameleon. No bigger than a fat sparrow, it blinked and swallowed a lizard whole. I've nearly died laughing at the creature. We brought it to table and it turded in F.'s salad; it sits on your finger and squeaks like Peggy does when she gets tipsy. I'll probably be taking it to bed with me, like Buff, when I first get tipsy. (NO I haven't been tipsy since I left NY.)

I s'pose Bina has already told you the details of the parental wedding in NY. Those last three days in town were mad ones for me. Cecil Fiske, Agnes' sister, gnawed at my hand for quite a while at the dinner with the Cowleys. I don't remember what it was all about but I think we fell in love with each other. I finally brought the bridal pair to lunch with Lachaise and Mme. A good time was had by all. L. insisted on my bringing the famous bird with me. All my fears about the trunks were wrong; they brought everything in fine shape, even china unbroken.

I feel like a gastric museum at present, a cross cut of Tahitian stomach coast — but not in especial distress — at least so far. Uric acid won't have a whispering chance in a few days, what with all the strange fruits and vegetables I'm trying. Casavas, guavas, breadfruit, limes, cumquats, kashew apples, coconuts, wild oranges, bananas, God I can't remember any more of the damned names. O yes, mulberries and avocados and papayas! And mangoes! Maybe I don't get enough of it yet! Tamarinds and pomegranates . . . grabanas . . . O sacre Nom de . . .

Please tell Mrs. Turner that I'll write her soon. I'm trying to get a few letters on the first boat. Tell her to put the above box number on my mail instead of "Casas Villa."

Love, hart

My mother finally said she envied me, going to the island — and the only time we had an argument was after the second act of *The Great God Brown* — which left us in a bad state.

The setting. — In *Letter #8* Hart is looking forward to the Cowleys' arrival as neighbors on May 1, yet on May 7 he is far away on the Isle of Pines near Cuba. His way of living had differed too much from that of the Tates for a joint board to be feasible for long. Mrs. Turner, very much under Hart's spell, had taken over preparing and serving Hart's meals in his rooms, where she joined him, adjusting herself to his hours and whims. "Mr. Crane's *so* sensitive and nervous," she would say admiringly. The house-sharing had not worked out well.

Both Tates and both Browns were busy at their typewriters trying to earn a living, in addition to having the usual indoor and outdoor tasks. With some justification, Hart felt he was working on *The Bridge* even when playing records, or tossing off cider and conversation in front of the Browns' fireplace, or just roaming around. He kept the wood-path between Addie's house and ours well tramped down, even in deep snow, turning up almost every afternoon for talk and mugs of cider. For "talk" was principally what he required of us. He was doing a vast amount of selective reading — Marco Polo's *Travels*, the Vedanta, everything he could put his hands on by and about Columbus and Captain John Smith. From such sources he sought support for his extraordinary vision of *The Bridge*. He tried out on us his ideas as they came to him. In retrospect, his time during this period seems to have been well used, for he hammered out the structure of *The Bridge* and created some of the detail. There were times when his friends felt as though they were the anvil on which he was hammering it out. His fellow-poet Allen bore the brunt. I cannot recall any tempestuous behavior from Hart during these months, nor any sustained drinking bouts. But we were not living with him.

Between the lines of a letter to Gorham Munson, written in early April, one can sense that Bill and Allen had tried to reduce the extent of the convivial talk in order to get on with their own work; Hart anticipated the arrival of Malcolm as a relief from ". . . the kind of shell that Brown and Tate seem to have retired into lately." By the middle of April Hart and the Tates had disagreed to the point where they could no longer remain housemates, and, in spite of Mrs. Turner's pleas, Hart felt that he had to leave. He wrote his mother the details of his dissatisfaction and received her reluctant permission to take refuge in Grandma Hart's villa on the Isle of Pines. He induced Waldo Frank to go with him.

By great good luck, plus a sincere sympathy with the predicaments of both parties and perhaps some discretion, Bill and I had managed to maintain affectionate relations with Hart. So, his bags packed and all travel arrangements made, Hart spent his last night in the country at Robber Rocks. We were to drive him to the early morning train to New York in our spring-rejuvenated flivver. Going out before breakfast, at dawn, to get water from the well, I saw, by a quick count, fifteen deer gathered around a water hole about one hundred feet away. I signaled Bill and Hart through the window, and they tiptoed out. The three of us stood watching the deer, who, catching our scent, stared motionless at us for a few moments, then broke and ran up the hill in single file to the edge of the woods. We watched them leap, one by one, with infinite grace, over the stone wall at its edge. Hart was transfixed; then he burst into tears and kept embracing us in turn, saying how much he loved us and would love us "till his dying day." We had trouble getting him into the Model T and off to the train; the country had again become alluring.

Reverting to the text of *Letter #9* — "Am. boats seem to be easy" refers to the now almost forgotten Prohibition Amendment. . . . The "National Winter Garden," a burlesque theatre on East Houston Street, was popularized in our circle by E. E. Cummings. . . . "— taking it to bed with me, like Buff . . ." Buff was our mammoth mongrel collie, whom Hart often lured home with him as an escort when he walked back through the dark woods at night. . . . "Agnes" was then Mrs. Eugene O'Neill, mother of Shane and Oona. . . . The "parental wedding" was Hart's mother's marriage to Charles Curtis in New York at the Little Church around the Corner. . . . The "famous bird" was the bronze cast of Lachaise's seagull, commissioned earlier, which from then on traveled with Hart almost everywhere, finally coming to roost on our mantelpiece at Robber Rocks. . . . ". . . don't get enough of it yet" is an example of Hart's liking for our "little language." A loyal defender of Eugene O'Neill, Hart had taken such vehement exception to someone's remark about Gene's "lolling" on Bermuda beaches that he became incoherent, spluttering: "Maybe Gene don't get enough of it yet!" — or so we said. His comeback was to make the remark his own; it occurs several times in these letters.

Letter #10.   To SJB.   From Nueva Gerona, Isle of Pines. May 22, 1926
Dear Sue:
The post-Crane period in Patterson seems to have been full of excitement. Your letter, with its news about the in-

comparable Jack, was corroborated in the same mail by no less than a letter from the noble tar himself. Poor Jack spent no little time and trouble, coming clear up from Norfolk. Mrs. Turner had been forwarding warnings of the impending disaster, first a letter from Norfolk on the date of landing, then a letter on the Potomac boat bound for Washington; I began to feel as though the wireless would be necessary to save my honor. His people live at Passaic and it was there, after his excursion north, that he finally got a card I had mailed from Havana, explaining things. He's back on the job now, but quits June 6th. I commend your control under the penetrating gazes of Mrs. T. Jack's letter contained a closing greeting from " 'me' — John's sister Mary" — written in a very elegant hand, so I guess I'm well introduced when I come to Passaic. Anyway, he bane good company and I'm awfully sorry to have missed him.

Yesterday I got tight for the first time, on Bacardi. Cuban Independence Day. Falling in with a flock of goats on my way home (I was trembling at what Mrs. Sampsohn would say) I stubbed my toe and skinned my knee. Arrived home in a somewhat obvious condition; there was nothing to be done but have it out with Mme. Waldo having left last Tuesday night, we had it fair and square. It is now established that I can drink as much as I damned please. A couple of murdering desperadoes got loose from the penitentiary here recently — and I think she's glad to have my company. But she's so damned pleasant and considerate that I haven't any reason to think she doesn't like me on less fearful grounds. I'm rather jealous of Mrs. T's old love, the weather, though.

Yes, Marianne took the little specialty I wrote for her, and even proof has been corrected and sent back. This time she didn't even suggest running the last line backward. "Again" is in the May issue; I s'pose you've seen the happy mixture. I enclose an accidental calligramme committed this morning accidentally on my way to *The Bridge*. I'm convinced that the Mango tree was the original Eden apple tree, being the first fruit tree to be mentioned in history with any accuracy of denomination. I've been having a great time reading Atlantis in America, the last book out on the subject, and full of exciting suggestions. Putting it back for 40 or 50 thousand years, it's easy to believe that a continent existed in mid-Atlantic waters and that the Antilles and West Indies are but salient peaks of its surface. Impossible forever to prove, however.

I'm glad that Malcolm has had such luck. It's likely he's made for life — once he enters the Lorimer field; and the articles ought to be interesting, certainly the material is. Because Poole's book, *The Harbour*, was said to have been written while looking from the windows of 110 Col. Hts., I had the idea that it might contain something — and have just finished reading it, a thin-chested little affair if there ever was one! I wonder if McFee's books are quite so ordinary.

Tell Bill to hurry up — and the Cowleys to write. My love to Bina and Romolo.

As always   Hart

The setting. — Mrs. Turner had appealed to me to drive Hart's uninvited caller back to the train, as she had no car. Hart's letter shows how pleased and flattered he felt at this evidence of real liking for him from his unlettered occasional drinking companion. There were no "penetrating glances" from Mrs. Turner. After his long trip from New York to Pawling and the ingenuity that he had shown in locating Mrs. Turner's, some six miles from the railroad station, the sailor was disappointed at missing the expected celebration of a long leave, for which he was prepared to pay, as he kept assuring us, in return for former treats.

". . . got tight for the first time": this was after the departure of Waldo Frank, whose dozen or so years of seniority and his constant high seriousness served as a restraint on Hart, an influence that unfortunately his more sportive younger friends did not possess to anything like the same degree.

60

The "calligramme" — a word that reflects Hart's reading of Apollinaire — was his first version of "The Mango Tree." The book Hart was reading was probably *The Problem of Atlantis* by Lewis Spence, issued by Brentano's in 1925.

"Malcolm's luck" was a commission from the *Saturday Evening Post* to write a series of articles on the African slave trade, on which he had been assembling materials for a book. He never wrote the articles for the *Post,* but the book on the slave trade did appear, after a lapse of thirty-six years. It was *Black Cargoes,* written in collaboration with Daniel P. Mannix. This remark is typical of Hart's constant response to the successes of his friends and his always ready concern for their welfare in every way. In spite of his growing bitterness over his own problems, and his gift for devastating ridicule when he thought it called for, he seemed to be devoid of envy.

Letter #11. To WSB and SJB. From Isle of Pines. July 14, 1926.
Dear Torarians and Banditti:

The gust and gist of your late news was very welcome, albeit I was laid up at the time with a double-barreled nonpareil earache, which time has since modified, however, to such an extent that I can now resume my eavesdropping at all the Gerona sewing circles and klatch-klubs. This was not accomplished without a trip to Havana where I was assured by a good-old-Columbia MD that I had neither boils nor abscesses, but that my oral or rather oracle receptacles had suffered such a splendid stewing, roasting and general sun-basting during my recent voyage that it might be some time before the cartilaginous contusions subsided. Out of which I have learned that a golf cap hardly fills the bill down here; the sun diddles one's brains anyway, through the widest straw.

Though I have probably passed off (and over) my agonies somewhat more modestly than you report Captain

Boving as doing "his" — I'm sure you'll appreciate what pains and sacrifices are involved in my even lifting an eye or finger to the typewriter after such throbbing days and nights. You will therefore be kind enough to assure Peggy of my best intentions — and that I'll answer her recent letter as soon as possible. Meanwhile I enclose such news from Nancy (transmitted through the Havana Post) as I am sure will afflict you all, and especially Peggy, extremely. Alas, that the dear little doctor should not have survived to hear the supplications of one of his devoutest patients only *one more Fourth* after the one I witnessed *chez* Brown! If Independence Day doesn't henceforth become "bitterer and Bitterer" for some of us I shall be surprised. You must recount to me all the accidents and vicissitudes of your multifarious celebrations. You already know mine — after six bottles of Tropical I sent you the wireless postal.

I am also sending you some scandalous news about Emil — which I have kept hushed in my file as long as I can bear it. Really, the newspapers contrive to keep one constantly stirred up, and I don't know how much longer I shall even open them. There seems to be no danger of jh sending me my copy of the LR, though — and I wish you would send me the complete evidence of all the wreckage she has made of my *Voyages* as soon as convenient. Nor have I received so far any official confirmation of the book's acceptance. It was nice of you to write me the details, and I've no doubt about the finality of the matters — especially as I get a like report from Frank. I shall take your advice and muster the due appreciations and the proper esteem for my publisher. He is probably much more tolerant than the NY Times will be.

Thinking that maybe you don't get enough ot it yet, I have looked in my ditty box and find some extra prints and snaps of the famous cruise. You will notice the intense pallor of "Captain Charley" perched on the poop, as well as fleeing visions of a frolicsome porpoise (harder to snap than to spear, by the way) on his way to visit M. Lachaise. But I must leave you now; baby grand is calling for Palestrina,

and I must tickle other keys. Let me urge you to a prompt
response and commit myself in the flattering subscription
of Mr. Jonathan Wild as

               adwhoringly yours,   hart

The setting: — The "gust and gist of your late news" refers
to my writing to him, early in July, a report that came to
me from Jimmie Light, to the effect that after much shilly-
shallying and much pressure, especially from Waldo Frank,
helped by Jimmie, Isidor Schneider and Gene O'Neill,
Horace Liveright had finally agreed to publish Hart's *White
Buildings* and had telephoned his printer in the presence
of O'Neill and Light. The delays, the blowings hot and
cold, had a devastating effect on Hart, alone on the Isle of
Pines after losing Frank's encouraging companionship and
his restraining influence. He began to feel embarrassed in
writing to his family, thinking that they would no longer
believe his "boasts." He even had to reassure Frank, who
seemed to think that the news in my letter implied that the
main credit for Liveright's final decision to publish went to
O'Neill and Light. Hart wrote to him: ". . . you must know
how little I credited the Light gossip; I simply thought you'd
be interested in hearing the sort of thing that goes around."
Frank's labors on behalf of the publication of *White Buildings* with Liveright and other publishers exceeded those of
anyone else. Nevertheless, for practical reasons, Liveright
held out for public endorsement of some kind from Eugene
O'Neill, whose name was much more widely known to the
book-buying public than Frank's. And Light's effective production of the Liveright-sponsored *Hamlet in Modern Dress*
with the late Basil Rathbone had created a stir that pleased
the publisher. The eventual compromise satisfied him:
O'Neill wrote a blurb for the dust-jacket, and Allen Tate
wrote and signed the preface, after generously offering it for
O'Neill's signature. The O'Neill blurb was used only on the
first edition of five hundred copies. Unmistakably O'Neil-
lian, it reads: "Hart Crane's poems are profound and deep-

seeking. In them he reveals, with a unique power, the mystic undertones of beauty, which move words to express vision." — copied from the jacket of a presentation copy inscribed: "For Bill and Sue — with my love always — Hart." Reading this, one understands why O'Neill resisted writing a preface to a volume of poems he liked without knowing why. O'Neill had told Liveright that, by insisting on an O'Neill preface, he was preparing a fine opportunity for O'Neill to make a fool of himself.

The "scandalous news" about Emil was a story in a Danish newspaper attributing a dedication to "E.O." in one of Cummings' books as referring to Emil Opffer, an obvious confusion in some Danish journalist's mind between the poetry of Crane and that of Cummings. Piqued by what he regarded as Emil's neglect of him, Hart misinterpreted this as having been inspired by Emil, as he was led on to do by the person who sent it to him. "E.O." in the Cummings' book was his first wife, Elaine Orr. . . . "jh" (as she signed herself) was Jane Heap, co-editor of the *Little Review* ("LR").

The "famous cruise" was a trip in a sailing schooner to Grand Cayman, during which Hart suffered so much from sunburn. "Captain Charley" was as black as he could be. . . . "porpoise . . . on his way to visit M. Lachaise": on several occasions Hart referred to the curvaceous M. and Mme. Lachaise, especially when seen walking side by side, as having the undulating grace of the porpoise, lines which occurred often in Lachaise's sculpture.

Letter #12. To MC and PBC. From Nueva Gerona, Isle of Pines. July 29, 1926
Dear Malcolm and Peggy:

I've been wanting to tell you how glad I've been to know about your good luck with the Post business, etc. — but you probably know by this time what I've been going through with. . . . There's really no news except that I'm better and have begun to write — for a period until pros-

trated by the heat — like mad. Columbus has been cleared
up — and a lot of other things started within ten days.

In the middle of the Bridge the old man of the sea
(page Herr Freud) suddenly comes up. I enclose this section, hoping you'll like it. Please mention or display it to no
one but Allen and les Browns for the time: it makes me
nervous to have parts of an unfinished drama going about
much before the curtain goes up.

It happens that all the clippers mentioned were real
beings, had extensive histories in the Tea Trade — and the
last two mentioned were life-long rivals. Rather touching.

Write when you get time,   Love — hart

Comment: Hart's enclosure was the poem "Cutty Sark,"
which became the third section of *The Bridge.* His mention
of Columbus reports his satisfaction with the completion of
"Ave Maria," the first section of *The Bridge.* Hart's creative concentration lasted well into October of 1926 and his
penned note on the back of a letter written to him by Malcolm from Sherman on October 8, 1926, shows that he was
already working on "The River":

Dear Hart: — I've spent the summer absorbed in two
operations — slaving over Valéry and lying on my
fanny to stare vaguely at the ceiling. "Septic condition"
was the temporary diagnosis, but my trouble turned
out to be a tumor on the bladder; there will have to be
a not very dangerous operation some time this winter.
Matty also is being operated on; mastoid in this case,
which is very serious indeed. . . . Today is one of a long
series of days when I meant to write you an immense
letter and didn't get around to it. I'll confine myself
to saying that I think The Bridge a magnificent piece
of work.

Here is a little joke. A ½ French and ½ American
poet named Eugene Jolas, modernist in his sympa-
thies, is compiling and translating an anthology of

modern American poetry, to be issued in Paris. He must have read my poems in the Little Review and remarked, "Ah, magnifique! Here is a bloat who has prepared a little anthology of my own and saved me a great deal of work." So he up and sends me a sheaf of questionnaires. I'm enclosing the one addressed to you. Walter S. Hankel also received one of these forms.

I thought seriously of letting Jolas remain in ignorance, and of having us all prepare fictitious biographies to send to him. But the joke isn't worth the trouble, and besides, you ought to be present in this anthology with a poem of your own. So I've explained his mistake to Jolas, and told him that I'm asking you to send some poem which you think easy to translate. Can't you select some piece from "White Buildings"? . . . What I'm going to do, God only knows. I'm dead broke, have to do a great deal of research and pay for an operation. Cripes. I wish I were living next to a breadfruit tree

> in savannas
> where bananas
> would grow all over me
> Jesus Christ how glad I'd be
> Yours — M.

Penned on the back of this letter, in Hart's handwriting, is:

That cricket never finishes, Uncle Stephen said —
When Aunt Sally smiled it was almost Louisiana

In *The Bridge* ("The River," Section II) Hart omitted Uncle Stephen and his cricket. This passage reads:

. . . I heard a road-gang chanting so
And afterwards (who had a colt's eyes) one said,
"Jesus! Oh I remember watermelon days!" And sped
High in a cloud of merriment, recalled

"— And when my Aunt Sally Simpson smiled," he drawled — "It was almost Louisiana, long ago."

In my fancy I can see Malcolm's bananas turning into watermelons, as befitted a "road-gang," and his savannas into the good old days in Louisiana, in a convict's recollection of how his Aunt Sally's smile created a sense of good living. Or am I being *too* fanciful?

Malcolm's "slaving over Valéry" refers to his translalation of a collection of Paul Valéry's essays. — To explain Malcolm's "little joke": the 1926 summer issue of *The Little Review* contained a group of poems by Malcolm under a general title, *Anthology*. Each poem was headed by the name of a poet, among them "Hart Crane," with the fictitious name, Walter S. Hankel, thrown in. The series was signed "Malcolm Cowley," but Jolas assumed that it was a bona fide "anthology" of seven poets, and sent his questionnaires to each.

Letter #13.   To WSB and SBJ. From Pawling, New York.   February 16, 1927
Dear Bill and Sue:

I left town last Sunday — so there was no time to see you again — and (already) scarce enough cash left to tip the conductor. The last two nights in town were mainly spent on the Hoboken waterfront, where you want to go (though it's for men only) if you want the good old beer, the old free-lunch counter and everything thrown in — for 15¢ a glass. Whiskey and gin are also much superior to the other side of the River and cheaper. Take the Christopher St. Ferry. Walk up *past* Front St. There are three in a row. Begin with McKelly's — or some such name.

The last night, went flying back to Brooklyn with a wild Irish red-headed sailor of the Coast Guard, who introduced me to a lot of coffee dens and cousys on Sand Street, and then took me to some kind of opium den way off, God knows where. Whereat I got angry and left him, or rather Mike Drayton did. Returning here to the home roost I found six cards from Jack the Incomparable with much more than the usual brief greetings, so Caramba!

Mrs. Turner was laid up all day Monday from an excess of oatmeal eaten at breakfast in celebration of my return. Went up to Tory Hill yesterday and found everything just as I left it. Encountered Mrs. Porwitzki at the Jennings and think she is marvelous. Did you ever talk to her? I never heard such locutions. I should love to tickle her. Since which I've been reading the Cock Also Rises (sent me by a Cleveland friend) and have developed a perfect case of acidosis. No wonder the book sold; there isn't a sentence without a highball or a martini in it to satisfy all the suppressed desires of the public. It's a brilliant and a terrible book. The fiesta and bullfight best. No warmth, no charm in it whatever, but of course Hemingway doesn't want such.

Love,   Hart

The setting. — The long interval between *Letter #11* and *Letter #13*, to the Browns, was due to the loss of several other letters, and to one of the upheavals that dogged Hart's life. This time, the agent was Nature, not Man. "From hurricane to blizzards, all in six weeks," he wrote Mrs. Simpson early in December, from Mrs. Turner's. In late October of 1926, a terrific hurricane almost demolished Grandma Hart's villa on the Isle of Pines. Hart had had a prescience of some kind of disaster. Starting in July, he had been sending everything he wrote on *The Bridge* to Waldo Frank for safekeeping. "I still must ask you to keep the enclosed somewhere," he wrote Frank on July 26. "One never knows what may happen, fires burn the house here, etc., and mss. be burnt or otherwise lost — and in the case of this *Bridge* I feel enough honor-bound to desire preserved whatever evidence of my industry and effort is forthcoming." What happened exceeded his fears. Shortly after the event, the Browns received a hilarious, still hysterical, description of how he and Mrs. Simpson

"Tomorrow I may find a room over on Columbia Heights if the patron saint of rooming houses (St. Anne, I believe) is feeling commodious." [*Letter #23*]

Hart Crane on the roof of 110 Columbia Heights, probably in the late fall of 1928. Courtesy of Columbia University Libraries Collection.

Photographic portrait of Hart Crane by his friend Walker
Evans, taken probably late in 1928, when he and Evans were
working together at Doherty's. Courtesy of Walker Evans.

"Photographs taken when the two were about the same age show a marked facial resemblance between Peggy Baird and Grace Crane."

Left: An undated photograph of Grace Hart Crane. She appears to be about forty. Courtesy of Columbia University Libraries Collection.

Right: Hart Crane and Peggy Baird in Mexico early in 1932. Courtesy of Columbia University Libraries Collection.

Photograph of an oil portrait of Hart Crane by David Alfaro Siqueiros . . . "whom I consider to be the greatest of contemporary Mexican painters. He's painted a portrait of me that is astounding." [In a letter from Mexico in November 1931] Courtesy of Columbia University Libraries Collection.

"During those winter and early spring months of 1924, Hart and I spent many evenings together when Jimmie was busy rehearsing The Spook Sonata *or* The Ancient Mariner *at the Provincetown Players."*

Left: Pencil drawing of SJB by Hart Crane, done early in 1924 in only a few minutes on the back of a Metropolitan Opera playbill for *Madame Butterfly,* in what Hart called Picasso's "fractured features" style. Courtesy of Columbia University Libraries Collection.

Right: SJB with her son Gwiffy at Agnes O'Neill's farm in Merryall Valley, Connecticut, in June of 1929. Agnes's niece Dallas stands in the background.

"The five of us spent a gay, silly Saturday afternoon, being photographed on postcards as cowboys and cowgirls in one of those odd shooting galleries on Times Square."

Left: From the left, Hart Crane, Allen Tate and WSB, late in 1924. *Right:* SJB (then Mrs. James Light), on the left, and Bina Flynn as cowgirls against the same background.

OPPOSITE PAGE

Top: The Browns' house, Robber Rocks, in New York's Dutchess County late in March of 1926. A light snow covers the house, the front of which had been painted white by Hart Crane the summer before. *Bottom:* Hart Crane, on the left, WSB and SJB in the Browns' $35 Model T Ford in the Bovings' driveway in Sherman, Connecticut, in the fall of 1925. Photograph by Paul Christian Lund.

"The three of us, Hart, Bill and I, stood watching the fifteen deer, who stared motionless at us for a few moments, then broke and ran up the hill, single file. We watched them leap, one by one, with infinite grace, over the stone wall at the edge of the woods. Hart was transfixed. He burst into tears, then kept embracing us in turn, saying he would 'love us till his dying day.' We had trouble getting him into the Model T and off to the early train.

"That winter, from Mrs. Turner's, Hart was keeping an eye on Robber Rocks while Bill and I worked in the City."

Left: Hart Crane in "fancy dress" in front of Eleanor Fitzgerald's house in Sherman, Connecticut, around Christmas and New Year's Day of 1926–1927. The girl was a Miss Silver, Fitzi's secretary at the Provincetown Players. Hart's "costume," including the malacca cane, had been his grandfather's. Photograph by Paul Christian Lund. *Right:* WSB, on the left, with Emil Opffer in front of Robber Rocks during the summer of 1930. Hart Crane probably took this photograph. Emil was visiting his mother, across the valley.

came through the storm alive as portions of the house collapsed about them, by shifting from room to room, both huddling under the same bed, covered with pillows, and then, as the storm waned toward dawn, crawling out and dancing madly to the tune of *Valencia*, pillows still on their heads. We were to expect him before long, he wrote. He spent a brief interval in New York City, where Bill and I were living and working that winter, and before the end of November had returned to his old rooms at Mrs. Turner's, the Tates having left by then. *Letter #13* reports one of his visits to the city, to break the monotony of his rural isolation, with no friends at hand either to cheer or to irritate.

"Mike Drayton": Hart told us that he often used the name of the Elizabethan poet as an alias on his tipsy prowls.

"Porwitzki": Mrs. P., our country neighbor, was the 250-pound mother of sixteen children born without the aid of a doctor. Of old local American stock, the Burch family, she had married an immigrant Pole. Hart introduced "Porwitzki" and other local references into the Quaker Hill section of *The Bridge:* the old Quaker Meeting House; the Adams' auction; Birch Hill, originally "Burch," up which Andy, the eagerly awaited mail carrier, drove to Mrs. Turner's. "Mizzentop" was the former grand hotel for the vacationing carriage-trade of the preceding century and for the occasional reunions of the prosperous departed Quaker families. Abandoned some years before our arrival, it stood mournfully on its commanding site at the high, central spot on Quaker Hill, awaiting destruction, a testimony to the callousness of changing tastes. Hart loved to prowl through its mouldy, echoing grandeur, stopping now and then to lean out through a broken window to take in the magnificent view over the Harlem Valley below, where the white church spires of the small town of Pawling showed through the old elms. Several times I drove him from Robber Rocks, two miles away on South Quaker Hill, to Mizzentop, and hung out the windows with him while he pictured for us the slow approach of the surreys and "rigs" of the mid-nineteenth

century, winding up the steep, rugged Quaker Hill Road.
He was later to describe it in *The Bridge.*

> Above them old Mizzentop, palatial white
> Hostelry — floor by floor to cinquefoil dormer
> Portholes the ceilings stack their stoic height....
>
> High from the central cupola, they say
> One's glance could cross the borders of three states;
> But I have seen death's stare in slow survey
> From four horizons that no one relates....
>
> Who holds the lease on time and on disgrace?...
> Where are my kinsmen and the patriarch race?...
>
> The resigned factions of the dead preside.

Letter #14.   To WSB.   From Patterson, New York.
           March 9, 1927
Dear Bill:
      There is a vague roar of snow water streaming the val-
ley so the roads may open soon if we don't have another
inundation. I've just come back from a moonlight tour of
Tory Hill — the Ford (with its ditty box and rear parts
quite gone) looks rather lonely. I was tempted to steal the
shovel lying in the coal pile, but desisted. Everything looks
well around the house — outside at least. The spring gur-
gles.
      I'm so glad to hear that Amos (or is it Trackle?) is so
well started! With only the 'beauty spots' to add, as you
say, you'll be fairly sure to have it ready for next fall's Liverwurst campaign. I may join you with a few fluttering pages
— if the muses hurry up a bit. Right now my prospects look
dubious.
      There is no particular news except the recent terrific
enlargement of Señora Turner (I hope you won't inflate
this mention into a myth of carnality on my part!) and I'm

much tempted to recite her the limerick on the young lady from Thrace, where belly rhymes with Nelly, etc.* She is knitting a crimson scarf for her next winter's use which Bloody Mary would envy and the Arno twins would rise from the page and grab if they weren't so busy on the hillsides culling posies these days.

Give Malcolm my best — and all at the celebration. I hope you and Sue decide to come out to the woods fairly early, however uncertain the prospects of my continuance here are. But you probably don't need urging.

as ever   Hart

The setting. — From Mrs. Turner's, Hart was "keeping an eye" on Robber Rocks while Bill and I worked in the city, living on Brooklyn Heights. If he had gone inside the house, he would have found his "darling little unreliable Everyman's Encyclopedia" a mixed-up mess on the floor, as we were to do in a week or so. During that fall and winter I had again been editing a pulp magazine, *Sweetheart,* while Bill alternated work on "Amos" and "Trackle," working titles for unfinished novels; a portion of "Amos" had been published in a 1923 issue of *Secession.* . . . After the agonizing over *White Buildings,* Horace Liveright had become "Liverwurst" to Hart. . . . The impending "celebration" to which Hart refers wistfully from his rural loneliness was a *bon voyage* party for Bill and me on the eve of our sailing for Jamaica on a banana boat. This inexpensive vacation had been arranged by the ship-wise Emil Opffer, then living on shore. The party was at the Hotel Brevoort suite of Lawrence and Peggy Guggenheim Vail, one of a series given by Lawrence during the Vails' sojourn in New York. On this occasion, Allen Tate went there with Bill and me.

*There was a young lady from Thrace
Who attempted her corset to lace.
    Her mother said: "Nelly,
    There's more in your belly
Than ever came in through your face."

71

As we walked along Macdougal Street enroute to the Brevoort, an Italian vendor approached us, holding a brown paper bag of small snakes in his hand, heads protruding like an animated bouquet. "Buy pretty green snake — just two bits." In those pre-marijuana, pre-LSD days, this was a startling sight on Macdougal Street. I am no snake-lover, but Allen apparently is, for he bought one and put it into his coat pocket. Pleased with his purchase, he exhibited it at the party and was promptly bitten. Turning as green as the snake, he dropped it onto the floor, where it slithered around panicking the ladies. A few of the men made a big to-do of putting a tourniquet on Allen's arm. At this point the maternal grandmother of the Vail children arrived; she fell into a panic of fear for the safety of her grandchildren. The problem then was how to dispose of the snake to pacify her. It was solved without immediate recourse to brutality. All this took time, so it was three o'clock in the morning when Emil saw Bill and me off to the banana boat in the East River. As we pulled away from the dock an hour or so later, the ship was rammed by a passing tug, a worse experience than the snake. The ship limped out to the Statue of Liberty, where we spent the rest of the day balancing ourselves on the inclined plane of the deck, while the captain bargained with a fleet of ship-salvagers. At dusk we were towed into drydock in Brooklyn, a block away from our vacated apartment.

Feeling sheepish about our "farewell" parties, we slunk away to Robber Rocks, driven up by Bina and Romolo, to await our next sailing date several weeks off. Hart welcomed us with zest and celebrated our escape from "death's door" by applying himself heartily to the hard cider in our cellar, then at its sparkling prime. Back at Mrs. Turner's, still stimulated by the cider and a lively discussion about President Calles of Mexico, Hart attempted to type a letter of commendation in Spanish, a language that neither he nor his typewriter knew. Annoyed with the balky machine, he threw it out his second-story window. During its descent the ribbon twined itself tenaciously around the boughs and branches of a large oak where, for a year or so, it waved in the breezes, especially visible on the bare boughs of the cold season, a reminder to beware of hard-cider enthusiasms, or at least their expression in Spanish.

Returned to Robber Rocks from our Jamaica trip in April, we were Hart's close neighbors until early fall. Each morning either Bill or I went to Mrs. Turner's crossroad to pick up the mail; most afternoons Hart turned up at Robber Rocks for croquet, our ruling passion that summer. At mail-time Hart often read to me drafts of his more ambitious letters, pretending to seek counsel, but in fact hoping that I would savor his phrases as much as he did. One day he watched for me in the kitchen door, eager to read his long letter to Yvor Winters (May 29, 1927) in which he castigates both Winters and Edmund Wilson — Wilson for a recent article in *The New Republic* ("The Muses out of Work") lamenting that contemporary American poets no longer played a large role in world affairs, serving as ambassadors, and so on, as had their predecessors. One phrase of Hart's letter referred to an earlier experience that he and I had shared: "It is so damned easy for such as [Wilson], born into easy means, graduated from a fashionable university into *a critical chair overlooking Washington Square . . .*" He emphasized the underlined words, then: "Remember? Remember?" he cried, laughing. And indeed I did remember. It had happened during the days when Allen Tate and I were both working on *Telling Tales,* Bina Flynn on our sister magazine *Ranch Romances,* and Hart on *Sweet's Catalogue.* We four office slaves, plus Bill Brown, had enjoyed a leisurely Saturday afternoon lunch, after our morning's work, at an Italian restaurant on Macdougal Street. Spurred on by Hart, we had decided to waste the afternoon on an expedition to Times Square — "just for the hell of it." So we strolled toward Washington Square and the bus terminal. Wilson and his first wife Mary Blair (another schoolmate of mine from Pittsburgh's Peabody High) at that time lived in the parlor floor of Number 3, Washington Square North; its wide front windows overlooked the Square. "Let's take a look at Number 3," Hart urged. "We'll probably see Bunny sitting at his work table in the front window, heavy learned tomes stacked high at both elbows, his hair ruffled and face red from expenditure of pure intellectual energy, scribbling away, giving his fine mind no week-end respite, oblivious to the outside world. Let's do an Irish jig in front of him." (Something like that.)

The sight that met our eyes at Number 3 corresponded closely to Hart's description. We pulled Hart away before he could break into an Irish jig and ran to the bus.

Enlivened by this incident, the five of us spent a gay, silly afternoon, being photographed on postcards as cowboys and cowgirls in one of those odd shooting galleries on Times Square. One photograph has Hart, Bill, and Allen posing as Dead-Eye Dicks against a background of a low Wild West saloon, with such signs on the bar-mirror as "Lodging by Night, Week, or Hour" and "This is No Man's Land — Come in and *START* Something." Another shows Bina and me wearing "chaps" and sombreros against the same background.

An earlier draft-letter that Hart had shared with me at mail time was the now famous "explication" of his "At Melville's Tomb," written to Harriet Monroe, the founder and editor of *Poetry,* and published in the October 1926, issue of *Poetry,* in which the poem first appeared. Before leaving for California in the fall of 1927 Hart clipped the pages of this letter from *Poetry* and mailed them to us, with this note penned in his neat, graceful handwriting: "Bill: — Will you please keep this somewhere for me? I don't remember your having read it at the time I wrote it —" It is now used in courses in American poetry as a text in "how to" read a poem.

Letter #15.   To SJB and WSB.   From Columbia Heights, Brooklyn.   October 11, 1927
Dear Sue and Bill:

As things look now I'll be off for Martinique on the 20th. Have made my reservation, in fact, and hope to get a

74

passport in time. Landa, the passionate poet of the seven veils, is already there, so I hear from Kathryn K. And there seems to be some chance of K. herself going. Times are bad already in NY, and it would only be a few weeks before I'd be down to just where I'll have to begin after coming back from M. — but without the breadfruit and the champagne for the meanwhile.

I'm wondering if you'd mind parcel posting me a few things. The two white dungarees and the one blue, also the soiled grey suit I wore around the country this summer. And the Bennet's French grammar (I think on my main bookshelf) if you can slip it in. There's a kind of telescope suit case (paper composition with strap) in my closet that would do to send them in.

Wish I could see you again before going, but don't think I can afford an expedition up. I'll write again soon, however. Aren't passport photos a scream? Even Lindy's face on the wall of the one I happened into looked funny. Arnold Wiltz nearly killed me last night with some abominable apple jack from Woodstock. He says Aunt Nelly mounted up to 275 lbs. and finally died. Love, Hart

The setting. — We had reversed situations since *Letter #14:* Hart back on Brooklyn Heights, and Bill and I at Robber Rocks. Hart had been living for some time on a monthly check of $50 from his father. While still at Mrs. Turner's and dreading the fall and winter job-hunting in New York, he had written to Otto Kahn asking for a loan to enable him to work in a mild climate for the winter. He enclosed everything he had written so far on *The Bridge,* much of which had been published in literary magazines, along with a detailed statement of his structural outline and general purposes, a document that adds much interest and pleasure to a reading of *The Bridge.* For instance, on the "Cutty Sark" section — "a phantasy on the period of the whalers and clipper ships," he wrote to Kahn. " 'Cutty Sark' is built on the plan of a fugue. . . . The airy regatta of phantom clipper ships seen from Brooklyn Bridge on the way home is quite effective, I think. It was a pleasure to use historical names for these lovely ghosts. Music still haunts their names long after the wind has left their sails." It is indeed haunting music — *Cutty Sark, Thermopylae, Black Prince, Flying Cloud, Rainbow, Leander, Nimbus, Taeping, Ariel* — stirring up memories of the China Trade of our forefathers' times, which scattered through so many American homes its mementos of strange Oriental objects. Kahn summoned Hart to New York and advanced him $300 for boat fare to Martinique. But Hart had to make an emergency trip to Cleveland, to help his mother and grandmother to pack and get off to California for the winter. This interruption changed his plans. He went back to Addie Turner's for several weeks' recuperation. The dreaded job-hunting followed, yielding him a job in a bookstore. Nothing more was heard of Martinique.

"Arnold Wiltz" was a painter, of Woodstock, New York, whom Hart had met during his winter there with Bill and Nagle in 1923. "Aunt Nelly" was one of the local characters.

Letter #16.   To WSB and SJB.   From Columbia Heights, Brooklyn, November 16, 1927, alias 2160 Mar Vista Avenue, Altadena, California.

Dear Bill and Sue:

Traintime approaches, but I hope life does not grow accordingly more hectic, as has been the rule so far! Several times I have all but lost my ticket, presented several days ago. Notably Tuesday night, in jail.

After a riotous competition with Cummings and Anne in which (I don't *know* but I'm sure) I won the cocktail contest, I found myself in the Clark St. station along about 3 o'clock playing with somebody's lost Airedale. The cop who rushed at me, asking me what I was doing, is reported to have been answered by "why the hell do you want to know?!!!" in a loud tone of voice, whereat I was yanked into a taxi and was sped to the station (slyly en route tossing all evidence such as billet doux, dangerous addresses, etc., out the window) and the next I knew the door crashed shut and I found myself behind the bars. I imitated Chaliapin fairly well until dawn leaked in, or rather such limited evidences of same as six o'clock whistles and the postulated press of dirty feet to early coffee stands.

I was good and mad. Made an impassioned speech to a crowded court room and was released at 10 o'clock sharp without even a fine. Beer with Cummings in the afternoon which was almost better than evening before, as C's hyperbole is even more amusing than one's conduct, especially when he undertakes a description of what you don't remember. Anyhow, I never had so much fun jounced into 24 hours before, and if I had my way would take both C'gs and Anne along with me to heaven when I go.

The Breughel is a belated wedding memento which I hope will bring warmth to your lips and a smile to your hearts occasionally. Had dinner with Isidor and Helen last night — who asked to be remembered. I don't know your 'new' address, so you must write me soon and let me know. Mine is included above.   Love,   hart

The setting. — Hart had been grouching to his friends about his physical and mental sufferings in the small, dimly lit bookstore. When Fitzi was consulted by a well-to-do broker friend as to a suitable companion for a six-months' stay in California, she suggested Hart, out of kindness to him and thinking that he met Herbert Wise's desire for a companion who would share his interest in music, art and literature. I had met Wise, a frail, quiet, reticent man. To me he and Hart hardly seemed compatible. The "train-time" that approaches will see Hart off to Altadena, for which, on November 17, he would leave with Wise, "his valet, chauffeur and 3 dogs." His mother, already separated from Charles Curtis, was then living in nearby Hollywood with her ailing mother.

Anne Barton was Cummings' second wife, former wife of Ralph Barton, the well known illustrator and cartoonist who had ended his life by his own hand. The Clark Street subway station is a few blocks from Columbia Heights. Hart's usual braggadocio is evident; he could not have taken his jailing as lightly as he told it. He was in fact extremely sensitive to the dirt, vermin, and disorder to which jails exposed him. This arrest is the first on record of a series stemming from the same cause, misbehavior when intoxicated — in Paris, in Marseille, several times in Mexico.

Isidor Schneider, on the editorial staff of Horace Liveright and a poet and novelist himself, had stood manfully by Hart in the *White Buildings* struggle. A year later he was to be my colleague at the Macaulay Publishing Company, where we both worked on issues of *The American Caravan,* some of which included portions of Hart's *The Bridge....* Our "new address" was a comfortable cottage on the Squibb estate in Bernardsville, New Jersey, to which we moved in late November to avoid being snowed in at Robber Rocks, and to have easy access to the New York hospital in which our son Gwilym was born in February of 1928. My kind friends Olga and Noyes Collinson, who lived nearby, had made arrangements for us.

Letter #17.   To WSB.   From Breakers Club, Santa Monica, California.   December 19, 1927

Dear Bill:

Yes, one can hear the sea seven flights below — and I've been walking on the beach most of the day. The boss, finding that I didn't get along any too well with some of his Hollywood week-end guests, advised my taking a vacation and with means happily provided here I am until tomorrow night. Wall Street seems to carry a slight oppression and madness with it wherever it "extends." It has been good to come over here where places are rather deserted of crowds and hear the gulls cry overhead and watch the solemn pelicans eye you a while and then haul up their legs and sprawl into the air.

Viennese cooking with caviar and port every night for dinner is playing hell with my waistline — and I sleep as never before, excepting the cradle. One can't seem to wake up out here without the spur of scotch or gin. There has been plenty of that — in fact last Saturday night I danced the "Gozotski" right on Main St., Los Angeles, while . . . an aviator . . . danced the Highland Fling or as good an imitation of it as he could manage. This after having invaded the Biltmore ballroom and dancing with fair ladies of the haute mondaine. Albeit — and having got our waiter drunk and having left in high dudgeon — I don't think I'll dare attend their supper club again.

After a good deal of fair "sailing" since arriving here — I am now convinced that "flying" is even better. Right now, however — and until next week-end — I am "all fives" on the ground and life can run as high as it wants to over in our villa without my batting an eye. And it *is* running high, I can tell you; that's why I'm here just now. . . . I never could stand much falsetto, you know.

God! You never know who you're meeting out here. . . . First there was a snappy collegiate hanging around the studios, who turned out to know Allen — and then today on the beach a mile below here, at Venice, I found myself talking literature, Spengler, Kant, Descartes and Aquinas — to say nothing of Charles Maurras and Henri Massis — to a Bostonian of French descent who knows Stewart Mitchell, and especially his aunt, very well! He turned out to be one of the best scholars I've ever met — a great reactionary toward the same kind of classicism that Eliot and Lewis are fostering in England. I had him spotted as a Romanist in less than five minutes — but he wouldn't admit it until we parted. The dialectic we had was more rousing than the aforesaid tonic combustions of alcohol, I admit.

Winters and wife will be here visiting relatives during Christmas week — and I look forward to that as a real event. Really, it's terribly dull having so many servants around, so much food, so much tiptoeing and ceremony. But it takes some of these Hollywood fays to revolutionize all that. Whoops! and whoops again, dearie, and then more warbling, more whiskey and broken crockery and maybe broken necks, for all I know, when I get back and view the ruins! (and please be kind enough to burn this page). The present "star" was once "Ariel" in the "Tempest" — and though she still makes the welkin ring I fear her voice would never do again. She has adopted the pronoun "we" to signalize her slightest thought, whim or act — and her conceit was so wounded on spying my "Chaplinesque" during the course of her drunken and exclamatory rampage through *Edificios Blancos* — that she nearly passed out and insisted on the spot that I make instant amends by composing a sonnet to her superb P.A. (Hollywood shorthand for "physical attractions") as displayed in her erstwhile success in "Peter Pan." Hence here I am by the sea — and mightily pleased — until the storm subsides.

My Spanish quotation from Slater Brown reminds me that I now have *Artista Adolecente* — a translation sent me by [Antonio] Marichalar who wrote a very interesting introduction. He was greatly interested in *The Caravan* and is going to review it in the *Revista de Occidente*. I must get started at my Spanish again. [I. A.] Richards' *Principles of Literary Criticism* is a *great* book. One of the few — perhaps the only one in English excepting stray remarks by Coleridge — that gets to bed rock. Weston's book, *From Ritual to Romance,* was quite fascinating — but Winters claims that scholars regard half of her data and deductions as imaginative bunk. Did I speak to you about Elizabeth Madox Roberts' new book — *My Heart and My Flesh* — before? Anyway, I hope you'll read it. I think it's a great performance.

Poor Addie! I got a doleful letter from her not long

ago — but she seemed to see *some* light in the improbable possibility of joining you in Bernardsville. I hope that plan will materialize. And how is Sue? Wish she would write when there isn't anything better to do.

I'm glad you liked the Breughel book. Its humor really belonged to you, if you get what I mean, and you therefore were more capable of "owning" it than anyone I ever knew. If you were dead and gone I think it would have been a better commemoration than flowers — so take good care of it — and hand it on to your grandchildren — for you never can tell — you may have them, you know!

Love always,   Hart

The setting. — "Gozotski" was Hart's favored phonetic spelling for this Cossack dance, as it was his favorite dance when exuberant. He performed it with extraordinary suppleness and dexterity, which few imitators could match. Allen is, of course, Allen Tate. Stewart Mitchell, an early editor of *The Dial,* had helped Hart over hard times in New York. Hart's correspondence with Yvor Winters, late poet and critic, has been mentioned. This was to be their first face-to-face meeting. *Edificios Blancos* was Bill's term for *White Buildings.* The "Whoops, dearie" passages are take-offs on Bert Savoy, a popular female impersonator of that time, a constant self-inspired subject of off-color humor, which Hart uses in a later letter. Peter Arno's "Whoops Sisters" had been cavorting in the pages of *The New Yorker* for some time. There was much "Whoopsing" going on in those days, in night-club circles and in the racier press. Hart's injunction to "burn this page" does his memory credit; but since most of it has already been published, it is too late to carry it out. But who can't see through this hyperbole to the much more humdrum facts given in a later letter? . . . Addie Turner *did* join us in Bernardsville, bringing with her "Toiger Titty Tat," as Hart called her mammoth pampered feline pet. Hart would be glad to know that the Brown grandson, Jason

Slater Brown, does exist. At the age of eleven, he lives up to any grandparent's fondest hopes. The Breughel book is still intact and Jason has put in his claim for it.

Letter #18. To MC and PBC. From California. January 31, 1928

Dear Peggy & Mal:

Writing is next to impossible — what with the purling of fountains, the drawling of mockingbirds, the roaring of surf, the blazing of movie stars, the barking of dogs, the midnight shakings of geraniums, the cruising of warships, etc., etc. not to mention the dictates of the Censor, whose absence will be welcome sometime, I hope, when we get together again at the Dutchman's or some rehabilitated Punch Palace where I'll at least be able to offer some new words to the (albeit) ancient tunes! My philosophic moments are few, but when they do occur it is almost always possible to turn on the radio and immediately expose my soul to the rasping persuasions of Aimee Macpherson, eternally ranting and evangelizing to packed houses at the great palm-flanked arena of Angelus Temple. She broadcasts the news that people are frequently carried out in pieces, arms broken, heads smashed in the stampede for salvation which she almost nightly stages, thereby emphasizing the need of arriving early (so as to save one's body as well) and thereupon lifts her voice into a perfectly convulsing chant, coaxing and cuddlingly coy about "Come, all ye —" (You can catch her in it on the Victor) the chorus of which would make a deacon's bishropric leap crimson and triumphant from the grave. I haven't seen her, but they say she has beautiful, long, red, wavy tresses.

The peculiar mixtures of piety and utter abandon in this welter of cults, ages, occupations, etc. out here make it a good deal like Bedlam. Retired schoolmarms from Iowa, Ohio, Kansas and all the corn-and-wheat belt along with millions of hobbling Methuselahs, alfalfa-fringed and querulous, side by side with crowds of ambitious but none-too-successful strumpets of moviedom, quite good to look at, and then hordes of rather nondescript people who seem just bound from nowhere into nothing — one can't explain either the motives or means of their existence. One can generally 'place' people to some extent; but out here it's mostly nix. One begins to feel a little unreal as a consequence of this — and so much more, like the perfect labyrinth of 'villas' — some pseudo-Spanish, some a la Maya (the colour of stale mayonnaise), others Egyptian with a simply irresistible amphora perched on the terrace, and some vaguely Chink. Our house, a large U with patio and fountain, rambles all over the place, and is almost vertical to the observatory on Mt. Wilson. Plenty of roses, camellias, oleanders, acacias, etc. as well as a good wine-cellar. I've just been interrupted by the butler bringing in a make-shift for champagne, composed of carbonated apple-juice with a sling of gin; so all attempts at epistolary consecutivety are hereby and henceforth abandoned! No, I'd better give up — I was just about to say something about the pool rooms down at San Pedro where the battle fleet rides close at anchor. Gradually I'm becoming aquainted with all the brands of bootleg that the Westcoast offers. I haven't been blinded by anything yet but beauty and sunshine, however; but I did have to get glasses to shield me from the violet rays, which are terribly strong out here. I'd better stop, I guess.

Love to you both, and peace to all our bladders! — Hart

Letter #19.   To WSB.   From California.   February 22, 1928
Dear Bill:

I am, above all, anxious to hear about Sue and the enfant sublime. My blessings — from the fairy God Mother in her native clime, here where the evenings are made lustful and odorous with the scent of lemon flowers and acacias on the sea-salt air!

A paean from Venusberg! Oy-oy-oy! I have just had my

ninth snifter of Scotch. O shades of Bert Savoy! They say he had a glass eye as the result of some midnight with a mariner. But I have had no such dire results as yet, OH BOy! Try to imagine the streets constantly as they were during that famous aggregation last May in Manhattan! And more, for they are at home here, these western argosies, at roadstead far and near — and such a throng of pulchritude and friendliness as would make your "hair" stand on end. That's been the way of all flesh with me. . . . And wine and music and such nights — WHOOPS!!!!!!!

Besides which I have met the Circe of them all — a movie actor who has them dancing naked, twenty at a time, around the banquet table. O Andre Gide! no Paris ever yielded such as this — away with all your Counterfeiters! Just walk down Hollywood Boulevard some day — if you must have something *out* of uniform. Here are little fairies who can quote Rimbaud before they are 18 — and here are women who must have the tiniest fay to tickle them in the one and only way! You ought to see [a well-known motion picture actress] shake her tits and cry *apples* for a bite!

What can I write about? Yes, I am reading Wyndham Lewis' *Time and Western Man,* Fernandez' insufferable *Messages* and all the other stuff. But I would rather do as I did yesterday — after a night of wine — wake up at dawn and dip into *The Tempest,* that crown of all the Western World. What have I to say after that event, I wonder???

> — The charm dissolves apace
> And as the morning steals upon the night,
> Melting the darkness, so their rising senses
> Begin to chase the ignorant fumes that mantle
> Their clearer reason. . . .

Maybe with me someday, as good Prospero says. Perhaps — as Ceres says in the same play —

Spring come to you at the farthest
In the very end of harvest.
Scarcity and want shall shun you;
Ceres' blessing so is on you.

But you will tear this up — and keep me true, Bill. And if I
come back to you and the dear hills of Connecticut again, as
I hope to, I shall have a cargo for your ears. My love to Sue
and to you.

as ever,

Hart

Enclosed is a souvenir of a night with Circe.
A most affectionate red-haired mariner — who brought
credentials.

The setting. — The "ninth snifter of Scotch" is the key to
this letter. It is made up of bits of Bert Savoy's and Mae
West's repertoires, with hints of Hart's own California life.
For one can't say: "I don't believe a word of it." Bill
brought this letter to me in the hospital about a week after
the birth of our son Gwilym. Hart was in serious trouble,
I thought; his stay in California could not last much longer.
As I put the letter aside, I looked up to the door of the cheerful hospital ward in which I was lying, almost expecting to
see him coming through it.

Hart's "throng of pulchritude" in this letter reminded
me of his tendency to impute his own responses to others. I
was walking with him in Times Square one day after a show,
when two loutish, pimply-faced lads in gobs' uniform passed
us, white hats squeezed down unbecomingly over one eye,
accentuating a moronic appearance. Hart seized my arm
and whispered: "Look at them, Sue! Aren't they bursts of
beauty!" Yet, it must be added, he understood the essence
of the man-woman relationship and the importance in it
of the protective man and the maternal woman. "What an
old fool André Gide must be!" he said to me after a talk
about two of Gide's books, referring to Gide's theme in *Cor-*

ydon and to his handling of Mme. Molinier's acceptance of her young son's corruption by a homosexual uncle in *The Counterfeiters*.

In this chaotic, seemingly self-indulgent letter a significant passage is the hope he expresses using Shakespeare's words that his "rising senses" would "chase the ignorant fumes that mantle clearer reason" — that he, too, would escape the threatening wintry death and move from harvest into spring. Repentance hovered, but he did not give himself up to it.

Letter #20. To MC and PBC. From 1803 N. Highland, Hollywood, California   March 27th, 1928

Dear Peggy & Mal:
    You're about as rapid as I am! I haven't heard from you since Christmas, meanwhile Mrs. Turner reports gloomy rumors about cysts and tumors. And it isn't that I owe *you* a letter!
    Have just seen Emil. We were both slugged and robbed in Pedro between drinks! The rest of the story is with Bill & Sue whom I've just written. Also just had my picture taken with Kahn at the Ambassador — some kind of news-reel. Look for me behind the horn-rims.
    Left the Wise mansion last week. Plan to remain out here, take up movie (scenario work if possible) and swell the family cash box. Nuff sed until you deign to answer my last. And please hurry. Please give my best to Hannah and Matty.
                                    Angrily,
                                        Hart

Letter #21. To SJB and WSB. From 1803 N. Highland, Hollywood, California   March 27, 1928
Dear Sue and Bill:
    As I don't seem to get anything more out of you by means of postcards, telegrams, and such-like shorthand sig-

86

nals I guess it's up to me to get busy on the typewriter and
pay you your due torture — though I'll try and not inflict
such piercing shrieks on you again, such as my last epistle!
When I get to feeling like that again I'll begin on Pres.
Calles first — and that will probably save you a good deal
of amazement and conjecture.

This time the news is more diverse. Life is nothing if
not exciting wherever Emil happens to land, if only for a
few hours. It took him (or his presence) to arrange the
most harrowing week-end yet, and I'm only praying that
he's still alive, for when I left him in his berth in the "glory-
hole" of the *California* last Sat. night he looked as though
he were nearing the Pearly Gates. We were held up and
beaten by a gang in San Pedro. The story is complicated and
lengthy — and Emil will probably give you the full version
or as much as he can remember when he sees you.

I left Wise's ménage a week ago today. However, as E.
somehow failed to get my ship letter announcing same and
the hour at which I would meet him — he flew right up to
Altadena, leaving me to wait a *full 8 hours* by the gangway
before I saw my dear "Goldylocks." By that time I had
about finished a half pint of alcohol which I had brought
for our mutual edification, and he had completely emptied
a quart of Bacardi, also originally intended as a mutual
benison.

Scene Two. Speakeasy joint with booths. Many bottles
of dubious gin and whiskey — with much "skøling" — Emil
flashing a fat payroll — and treating three or four still more
dubious "merry andrews" who had invited themselves to
our noisy nook. It being midnight, all ordered out.

Scene Three. A street, or rather, several streets. Our
"guests" very insistent on taking a hotel room in which to
finish the fire water. Emil & I both reeling but refractory.
I finally noticed Emil being spirited away by three of them,
while it was evident that I, who had been more emphatic
in my wishes, was being guarded by two others. I broke away
— and had just caught up to Emil who was being put around

a dark corner — when all five started slugging us. I put up quite a fight, but neither of us was in much condition. They all beat it as a car turned on a nearby corner. Both of us robbed of everything, and E. practically unconscious. After reporting at police headquarters, I don't know how I would have got E. back to his ship without the help of a sailor friend of mine whom I had run into earlier in the evening while waiting for E. We roused several of his shipmates — and I'm only hoping that his bumps and bruises haven't been any more fatal than mine. I finally had to finish the night in a ward of the Salvation Army Hotel, and it was five o'clock Sunday before I got enough money to get back to Hollywood. On his way back from Frisco I'm hoping to see E. again — but not in Pedro! Probably nothing of this had better be mentioned to the Bovings. . . . I don't mind my losses, but I feel terribly about Emil's luck. He always seems to get the hardest end of things.

As you can see, we didn't get much time for any gossip. But he did say that you had the most beautiful baby in the world! Wish I could see him! Besides which I get terribly homesick out here, but might as well not indulge myself in that emotion. My resignation from the Wise entourage was encouraged by a number of dissatisfactions, but as much as anything by the recognition of the fact that I must settle here for a while at least, and do whatever I can to help mother during her attendance on grandmother. The two of them being completely alone out here, and none too well provided for, I couldn't get a good night's sleep in Conn. So I might as well relinquish my own wishes for a while and try and earn some cash. Maybe scenario writing eventually. Meanwhile there are mechanical jobs such as title-writing, gag-writing, "continuity" writing, etc. I just had an interview with "Papa" Kahn this morning who is out here for a couple of weeks. He promises to help me connect with Lasky, Paramount, Wm. Fox, etc. At least I have "broken in" the movies in one way, for Pathe News Reel or some such torture swooped down on us while we were talking in the patio of The Ambassador, and for all I know we may be thrown upon the screen together all the way from Danbury to Hong-Kong and Mozambique! I'm wearing horn-rims now — so don't be shocked.

As for my late employer — the situation became too strained to be continued. If I had only had some definite duties I could have kept my self-respect, but the tip-toeing, solicitous, willy-nilly uncertainty of everything, besides his interminable psychoanalysis of every book, person, sausage and blossom got to giving me the heeby-geebies. And when he finally secured a quite cultured little piece of Pear's Soap (remember the slogan) to console him in all ways at once, then I began to feel too extraneous for words. Such circumstances don't promote a very lively morale — and it's probably better for me to lose a little of the attendant avoirdupois in favor of a more exhilarating outlook. But we are still friends so far as I know.

Every week I scour the pages of the New Rep., Nation, and Herald-Tribune for the names of our "rising generation." Have seen nothing by Malcolm for some time. Does this corroborate the news I got from Mrs. T. some weeks ago that Malcolm has been laid up? Much by Robert Penn Warren but little by his friend Tate, excepting a recent review of Winters which I thought excellent. Slater Brown, I long since neglected to mention, scored keenly in tussle with the milksop critic of Estlin C'gs in the Canby Crap Can. "The point was well taken," as my grandmother would say. And how is C'gs? — for I think you told me he was pretty hard up. Mitchell seems to be bursting with new energy by the evidence in recent numbers of The Dial. And last, but not least in this lit'ry column, how goes it with your translations — and — how is "Amos"? No, you're not the last, either! I must say that I haven't yet been able to decipher that defense of me by Laura, published in *transition* along with Kay Boyle's explosive boil. I wrote her promptly, thanking her for her sentiments, but questioning her style. Her latest book, announced by Jonathan Cape, is *Anarchy*

Is Not Enough — and so she seems to be maintaining her consistency. Judging by the time she has already taken before answering me, I judge that I'm off her correspondence list. I shouldn't have been so rude had I thought her tenderhearted. But I can't believe that anarchy is enough — or Gertrude Stein either.

I imagine you'll receive this at a rather busy period — re-settling in Patterson, swimming in the gully-torrents, planting the new garden and tripping over croquet wickets — but try to get me some words on paper somehow as soon as possible, for I'm devilish anxious to hear from you. My love to the bambino! — Yours ever, Hart

The setting. — The "piercing shrieks" may have referred to the bibulous abandon of *Letter #19* or to a later letter, long since lost, in which he complained bitterly about his mother. — "I'll begin on Pres. Calles first" is a reference to his earlier quarrel with his typewriter for refusing to write a letter in Spanish to the Mexican president. — "Goldylocks" as Hart's quotes suggest, was his teasing name for Emil Opffer, who as a young man had very yellow hair with a long forelock that tended to fall over his forehead. — ". . . Pear's Soap (remember the slogan)": we did, of course, for it was as common in 1928 as is "Tastes good like a cigarette should" forty years later. The words were: "He won't be happy till he gets it," and the illustration showed an infant in a tub of water, eagerly reaching out for a floating cake of Pear's Soap. — ". . . milksop critic of Estlin C'gs": Cummings' play *him* was produced at the Provincetown Players at about that time by James Light; the "Canby Crap Can" was Hart's usual term for the *Saturday Review of Literature,* edited then by Henry Seidel Canby. "Amos," it may be recalled, was the working title of Bill's novel-in-progress. — "Laura" was Laura Riding, the poet, referred to earlier, then living in England, where she and Robert Graves were to receive Hart warmly at Christmas in 1928.

Letter #22. *To WSB.* From Hollywood. April 27, 1928.

Dear Bill:

Your salute to the comments of the ny critics' cracks at *him* displayed more life than I have seen around here since I arrived. Although I am still holding my sides, I'm a little sad; for I would like to have been there. Especially with Anne drinking gin and Emil sporting his shiners and shirt front and all the tumult and guzzling there must have been afterward! As for the critics — C'gs can be envied, in the same manner that even I can be envied, whereby I refer to the "clever" handling I recently got from Benet in the Canby crap can. At least we both have managed to evade the proverbial faint praise! Your clipping was the only one I've seen excepting a letter from Dos in the last Sunday *Times,* and a laudatory review in the *Wall Street Journal* which Wise had noticed. I hope you and others will make as much of a controversy about it as possible. That's one good thing about Frank — he never hesitates a moment and never tires.

Since the Fleet with its twenty-five thousand gobs has left for Hawaii I have had a chance to face and recognize the full inconsequence of this Polyanna greasepaint pinkpoodle paradise with its everlasting stereotyped sunlight and its millions of mechanical accessories and sylphlike robots of the age of celluloid. Efforts for a foothold in this sandstorm are still avid, but I have had little yet in encounter. "Crashing the gate" is a familiar expression out here, and it seems to be exclusively applied to the movie industry. To cap the climax I have to endure my mother's apparently quenchless desire that I become an actor! But if I can hold on until the middle of May I'm due for an interview with Jesse Lasky (HIMSELF) and maybe through that entree I can creep into some modest dustpan in the reading dept. of Paramount. Your friend Dietz, by the way, draws a cool $750.00 a week as their ad. mgr.

It's good to think of you as back near Patterson. I had a

good letter from Malcolm. It all makes me homesick.
Things like that croquet game in the rain, the afternoon at
the cider mill, the skeleton surrey ride and the tumble
down the hill! I haven't a thing to send for the *transition*
Am. issue. I can't imagine ever having anything to say out
here except in vituperation of the scene itself. If I could
"afford" to go to work on some ranch it might be otherwise,
but that, under present circumstances, doesn't seem advis-
able.

Have just discovered the presence here of Mrs. Alice
Barney, the world-famous *grande dame* and mother of
Nathalie Clifford Barney of Paris, friend of Valery, trans-
lator . . . etc. As she is a great friend of Underwood of Washington I have been invited to her next "evening." She ought
to be a little different than the typical Hollywood hostess
— perhaps mildly Proustian. God knows I need some sort of
diversion besides bus rides and the rigor mortis of the local
hooch. Forgive this spasm and write again soon.   yrs   hart

The setting. — Thanks to the diversion of entertaining
news from the East, this letter, while far from cheerful, suggests a peaceful though not uncomplaining resignation to
his California exile, with only one mild crack at his mother.
Yet little more than a week later Hart was to write us his
most desperate of all the California letters — the second of
these letters that has disappeared.

Emil's "shiners" were the aftermath of the San Pedro
hold-up. Bill had written Hart a description of the custom-
ary opening night party at the Provincetown, parties that
were famous in their time for the wide variety of persons
who swarmed to them. They were held in the lounge rooms
above the tiny theatre, once a stable, on downtown Macdougal Street. I recall seeing among the assemblage at one
party, Scott and Zelda Fitzgerald (brought by Edmund Wilson); Eugene and Agnes O'Neill; three painters: Stuart
Davis, Glenn Coleman and Marsden Hartley or Charles De-
muth; Dr. Albert Barnes, the art collector of Philadelphia,

inventor of "argyrol," who was magnetically drawn to the three painters; the editor of the socialist Jewish *Forward*, Abraham Cahan; Alexander Berkman, the anarchist who shot H. C. Frick; and "Putzi" Hanfstaengl, who in later years was to play the piano to soothe the savage breast of Adolf Hitler. Hart was familiar with these gatherings, and Bill's account would make him homesick in his California isolation. Cummings' *him* would have attracted a good crowd.— "Dos" is John Dos Passos. — "Your friend Dietz" refers to a Columbia classmate of Bill's who was to rise high in the motion-picture industry, and, in latter days, to fall. — Natalie Barney, a well-off American and an associate of Gertrude Stein in Paris, was a patron of both French and American arts and letters during the "American exile" years in Paris. She gave Ford Madox Ford some financial support for his *transatlantic review*.

The Californian period was a catastrophe from which Hart never fully recovered. In his letters to us a kind of frenzy, abandon and desperation is revealed, almost a plea for rescue. *Letter #17* suggests the beginning of a downward slide. *Letter #18,* to the Cowleys, is the best he wrote from California, similar in tone to his best letters from the Isle of Pines. *Letter #19,* written when intoxicated, is the recurring note of Hart the sensitive poet, man of letters, and good friend, with discerning comments on what he was reading, affectionate concern for his friends in the East, and an indication that he still hoped to emerge from his growing need for alcohol and the forgetfulness of self in sensual indulgences.

There was a steady deterioration in his relations with his mother, and then the dismal end of his love for her. Mrs. Crane was living in a bungalow in an unpretentious section of Hollywood, with Grandma Hart and, for a time, another woman. Her brief marriage to Charles Curtis had ended in the divorce court. Hart had hoped for much from this marriage: happiness for his mother, peace of mind for himself. He had urged her to patch things up with Curtis: "I have the idea that you both care for each other more than you thought you did. . . . I've never been able to figure out what the quarrel was 'all about.' " In Hollywood Mrs. Crane was not in good financial circumstances, as Hart admitted even though he did hold her responsible for it. During Hart's twice-a-week visits to her from Altadena she poured her troubles on him. This threw him into a turmoil; he felt inadequate, guilty, and resentful all at once. Resentment finally triumphed.

His letters give various dates for leaving the Wise ménage in Altadena and settling in with his mother in Hollywood. It is likely that he tried out a short stay in Hollywood, then returned to Altadena, and found that equally impossible, in his vacillating state of mind liking neither the one nor the other. Having committed himself to the move, he attempted to put it in a good light, especially to Waldo Frank with whom, as usual, he put his best foot forward — a good son and grandson who could not feel "justified in leaving my mother and grandmother alone out here in their present predicament," and who sought a job in the movies so that he could be of some "substantial help." To us, also as usual, he gave a number of less righteous reasons for leaving Wise: "dissatisfactions" which he enumerates. In this conflict his reliance went more and more to alcohol in order to attain a bearable state of mind. After a few months of this he flew back to the devoted tolerance of Addie Turner.

There was a melodramatic final scene in his mother's Hollywood bungalow, in which mother and son hurled insults at each other. In his passion of revolt Hart accused his mother of causing *his* financial predicament as well as her own, and renounced all future responsibility for her. Even worse, he came out with his sexual deviance and blamed her for it, a step he soon regretted for its possible effect on his father if she revealed it. Then he surreptitiously packed and smuggled his luggage out of the house for immediate flight. That was the drift of a lost letter and his later story, as I recall it. After Hart's death, Mrs. Crane's version of this incident — as she gave it to Philip Horton, Hart's first biographer — differs from my recollection. The outlines are all softened; Hart is shown as telling his mother about his homosexuality in a calm, considerate manner aimed at reducing the shock of this unwelcome revelation; she recalled herself as receiving it with equal control. In her grief after Hart's death, this version is understandable; bereavement makes memory kind. However, it hardly seems to accord with the temperaments of either mother or son. He later wrote to the Rychtariks that he was forced to "steal off East like a thief in the night," and to the Schneiders, "I was mightily glad to get back among friends; I could find no work in California and excessively hysterical conditions arose between me and my family there. Altogether it was intolerable." And, after Grandma Hart's death the following September, Mrs. Crane refers in correspondence to a "vicious" telegram she had received from Hart to which, she admitted, she sent an "equally vicious" reply.

His letter of thanks to Waldo Frank, after his arrival at Mrs. Turner's, implies that he had wired for a loan to travel East. By mid-May he had entrained for New Orleans; from there he returned to New York City by boat. California had been a disaster for him.

During the next six months there was almost no correspondence between Hart and us, because from late in May until early in December of 1928, he was living near us, at first in the country and then in New York. Back from California and quite subdued, he had made a beeline for Mrs. Turner's. He found Robber Rocks given over to the installation of a bathroom, the construction of a large screened porch on the east side, work on translations proceeding, communal croquet every afternoon on our lawn, sometimes even in the rain; and, in the midst of all this, the constant care of a baby going on. Malcolm and Peggy Cowley were then living nearby, having bought their own house by that time, on the same road as Mrs. Turner's and just beyond the place of Eva Parker and her June-oh! But they kept a flat in New York, where Malcolm from time to time had to stay working on the various literary and publishing chores by which he earned their living.

Hart resumed work on *The Bridge* and patched up relations with his father, who sent him a check and advice. He was relieved to learn that his mother had obviously not disclosed his sexual deviance to his father. Often he jogged up the road from Mrs. Turner's the short distance to Malcolm's study, to encourage and discuss *Blue Juniata,* as Malcolm's first volume of poems was to be called when it was issued the following year.

Soon after his return to Mrs. Turner's, he resumed keeping a record of expenditures in the same notebook he had used for this purpose in 1926 and 1927. Some of the entries are reproduced here; they throw light on matters referred to in his letters. Hart left the notebook at Robber Rocks, along with books, a pair of snowshoes, and other belongings, when he moved from Mrs. Turner's to Fitzi's in July of 1930. Written on it in my handwriting is "Hart Crane's Notebook." Note that the entry for "June '28" shows that the date of Hart's return to Mrs. Turner's from California was about May 20, 1928. This accords with his report to the Schneiders in July that he had left California "about the middle of May." Hart's payments for room and board to Mrs. Turner in November and December of 1926 after his return from the Isle of Pines are also recorded. *Letter #13* to us refers to his stay in New York early in February 1927. There is also a recapitulation of expenditures during the winter of 1926–1927, some in the country, some in New York. Sam Schwartz was the proprietor of a restaurant-night club, the "T.N.T.," later called the Black Knight, on Macdougal Street opposite the Provincetown Players. Pagani's is still a record shop on Bleecker Street. Laukhoff was a Cleveland bookdealer from whom Hart ordered a copy of *White Buildings* for Charlotte Rychtarik in December of 1926. The Corona typewriter item shows the cost of repairs after the President Calles incident in March of 1927. Harrie Wright had a clock, watch, and jewelry store in Pawling.

By mid-August, Hart was again job-hunting in New

Excerpts from a notebook left by Hart Crane in his desk at Robber Rocks, in which he occasionally kept his accounts. Notations are in mixed pen and pencil, unmistakably in Hart's handwriting. The notebook is now in the Columbia Hart Crane Collection.

Accounts	June '28
	paid $12 for 2 weeks
Feb. 15, 26	ending Sunday June 3rd
Allen .... 8.75 plus 5	
Brown .... 5.00 plus 2.00	....
Brown .... 7.00 plus 4.00	Owing me
Brown 3.05	Malcolm 8.00

....	
Cleveland long distance	Boving .45
2.70 for 3 minutes	Star Oil 8.80
.70 for extra minute	Sam Swartz 15.95
.45 1 New York call	Wash. Sq. Bk Sh. 9.25
....	Laukhoff--
Owed to Brown	Harrie Wright 7.32
1.00	Corona Typewriter 15.00
.50 for typew. ribbon	
.25	Munson 5.00
5.00	
6.75	Pagani 2.25
....	Squarchialupi 5.15
Board and Room	
Arrived at Mrs. Turners Nov. 6	69.17
$13 .... and month's rent paid 13	
7. - board paid 20	
7.45 board paid 27	
9.00 board-rent paid Dec. 4	
first 2 weeks in Feb. absent in N.Y.	

York, living at first in the Cowleys' city flat. Four letters he wrote to Malcolm during the August–December period tell quite a bit about his life then. Their subject matter tends to be interlocking, so they are inserted here chronologically, with comment to come later.

Letter #23.   To MC.   From 501 E. 55 St., New York.
Near August 20, 1928
Dear Malcolm:
    Started in today on that agency job which I mentioned as looking probable, and tomorrow afternoon I may find a room over on Columbia Hts if the patron saint of rooming houses (St. Anne, I believe!) is feeling commodious. I may continue to use these quarters occasionally, however, as you suggested. Meanwhile, probably the best place for the key (I mean where you'll find it) is under the linoleum in front of the door. Let me know if you think better of other repositories. Mrs. Turner will know whatever new address I may have. Meanwhile, if you're in town soon, phone me at *Griffin, Johnson & Mann,* 18 East 48th St. It looks like a very decent outfit to me, but they may not have more than three or four weeks work for me at most. At any rate I've been taken in under the enthusiastic auspices of a former copy-chief of mine in Cleveland. I'm expected to perform prodigies, but I feel as rickety as a cashiered Varian. Maybe I'll limber up in a day or so. Of course they *would* put me to writing on wedding rings the first day!
    Doubtless by this time you have seen Fitzi. Lorna and I had dinner with her yesterday and heard all the dirt on Paris, etc. Lorna certainly, and I quite possibly—will be up your way on Labor Day. So the orthophonic may get back with me then. I really miss a tune now and then. Let me know what Harpers do about your country elegy. You know how I like it! And do more! And give my love to Peggy and the Browns.
                Yours ever,—Hart

Letter #24. *To MC.* From 110 Columbia Heights,
Brooklyn. October 24, 1928
Dear Malcolm:

I'm expecting to hear from you today or tomorrow. But in case you *don't* come in town until later, I'm writing to ask you to bring in all the mss material of your poems which I was in process of editing last summer. I'll soon have plenty of time to give the matter, and I have a suspicion that something will come of it now. *Main 2649* is the phone number. Lorna wants to see you, too. Best to Peggy.—Hart

Letter #25. *To MC.* From 110 Columbia Heights, Brooklyn. November 20, 1928

the 20th of the 28th at the A.M. 7-thirtieth
Dear Malcolm:

After the passionate pulchritude of the usual recent maritime houreths—before embarking for the 20th story of the Henry L. Doherty Co's 60 on Wall Street story—I salute your mss. which arrived yesterday morning—as well as the really cordial apologies accompanying them for the really unhappy hours inaugurated last week by the hysteria of S. God damn the female temperament! I've had thirty years of it—lacking six months — and know something myself.

It's me for the navy or Mallorca damned quick. Meanwhile sorting securities of cancelled legions ten years back — for filing — pax vobiscum — With Wall Street at 30 per — and chewing gum for lunch —

But here I am — full of Renault Wine Tonics — after an evening with the Danish millionaire on Riverside — and better, thank God, a night with a bluejacket from the Arkansas — raving like-a mad. And it's time to go to work. So long. . . . I'll be careful with the mss. And your book'll be out within 7 months. . . . About time! God bless you and give my love to Peggy! And as W. J. Turner says: "Oh hear the swan song's traffic cry!"

Letter #26.   To MC.   From 110 Columbia Heights,
Brooklyn.   December 1, 1928

Dear Malcolm:

It has been a pleasure for me to spend part of the last
two days in typing the mss. of your book. Certainly I have
been on more intimate terms with the poems than ever, and
my enthusiasm has been heightened thereby rather than in
any way diminished.

I now have two copies, one to turn over to the "secret"
arbiter here and one to take with me to England. Whatever
may or may not happen over there I'll at least be sure of
having you along with me — which is much. By the way, if
the mss. is returned to you, refused, be sure to send it at once
to Coward-McCann, who, I understand, are calling for new
poets and planning some kind of series of them. Hannah
spoke to me about this yesterday.

Although I hope to get off next Saturday (probably on
the Tuscania) I'm not at all certain. The bank behaves too
strangely — now ignores my letters not to mention telegram.
The meddlesome old nanny that is handling the matter
there will soon hear from me through a lawyer if things
don't take a new turn by Monday. That's the only way to
handle it, I guess. I'm to see Art Hays Monday and talk it
over. At any rate, I think it would be foolish to bring my
troubles over to London with me and have them poison my
first impressions of the place.

To get back to the poems: I omitted practically nothing but the Decorations. The arrangement you made is
ideal. As to the places for the following, I think you'll agree
that they are ideal:

Tumbling Mustard just before *Memphis Johnny*

Still Life just before *Seaport* (it doesn't fit in the Grand
Manner section particularly)

Two Winter Sonnets just after *St. Bartholomew* (they
come in eloquently there)

Really the book as we now have it has astonishing structural sequence. Most of the more doubtfully important
poems come in the central section. There is the fine indige-

nous soil sense to begin with in the Juniata, and the eloquent and more abstract matter mounting to a kind of climax toward the end. Hope you don't mind my enthusiasm!

See the Show Boat when you come to town. Wise took me last Tuesday night; the beautiful new Ziegfeld Theatre has them all beat — and the settings, songs, costumes and glistening lithe girlies! Like greased lightning — the suave mechanical perfection of the thing.

You may not hear from me again if I leave next Saturday, but Mrs. Turner will be informed when I leave anyway. I'll see that your mss. (the original) is remailed to you registered, early next week. Lorna and I went on the best bat ever last night — Sam's old place — finally two cops came in and joined the party at three o'clock — asked Lorna to marry me and live with me in Spain — but she's got to wait for her divorce from the Danish gaucho now on the pampas.

My love to you both, as ever — your — Hart

Letter #23. — "Your country elegy" refers to Malcolm's essay "My Countryside Then and Now," which was published later that year in *Harper's Magazine.*

Letter #24. — ". . . plenty of time" refers to the anticipated ending of his job.

Letter #25. — Hart's friend, the photographer Walker Evans, had found him a job in the filing department of the Henry L. Doherty brokerage firm on Wall Street. Even in this chaotic letter, obviously written while he was still feeling the effects of a night on the tiles, Hart's concern for Malcolm's poems is still to the fore.

Letter #26. — "Hannah" was Mrs. Matthew Josephson. Though his inheritance was not then settled, Hart had reserved passage for England on the *Tuscania,* on which he did in fact sail early in December. Though I had tried to dissuade him from a law suit against his mother, as there was a strong likelihood that the delay in settling was normal procedure, to appease him I had given him an introduction to my old friend Arthur Garfield Hays, whose judgment I trusted.

(A few years later, in 1933, Art was to become internationally prominent through his brilliant defense of Georgi Dimitrov in the "Reichstag Fire" trial.) The inheritance was soon settled, and without a suit. — Hart's reference to his proposal of marriage to Lorna Dietz sounds almost serious. Lorna's long-absent husband was the Baron Alexander Boije af Gennas, a penniless but pleasing Swedish-Finnish aristocrat who had appeared on our social scene through my Scandinavian friends. He was another example of Nordic *Wanderlust*.

"To get back to the poems," like Hart. Hart's last three letters refer to his concern with the preparation for publication of Malcolm's poems, to which he applied himself with rare devotion. I have asked Malcolm to write his own account of it.

A Note by Malcolm Cowley

After his disastrous long visit to California in the winter of 1928, Hart spent two or three of the summer months in Patterson. I had moved into the neighborhood that spring, having contracted to buy, if I could make the payments, sixty acres of abandoned farmland and a hungry-looking house half a mile from Addie Turner's. Like everyone else I noticed that Hart's bristly hair was turning iron-gray and that his face was redder and puffier. Those were signs of a physiological change, from being a "heavy social drinker," as we had always known him, to being a "problem drinker," the first stage of true alcoholism. He was paying more and more visits to Wiley Varian, the cashiered army officer who ran a speakeasy on Birch Hill. "Sometimes Hart gave a party," and then, says Nathan Asch, who was living in "the Tates' part" of Addie Turner's big house that summer, "we, the writers rejected by New York booming with the market of the twenties, consoled ourselves with the gaiety we could engender ourselves. We drank the liquor from either Varian's or one of the other bootleggers, and then we shouted and then we danced. . . . We did not speak to each other, but rather each of us howled out, and we did not dance with our wives or even with each other, but whirled around Hart's room, faster and faster, as if we were truly possessed." Yes, we did that and more, with the phonograph blaring and Hart leading the revels, but we did it on only one occasion; I think it was on his birthday, July 21. Hart was never much of a party-giver.

Instead he was a party-goer. He distinguished himself, though I don't remember how, at the Fourth of July party on Tory Hill, and he came back from New York City for the party on Labor Day. Everybody speaks of that summer in terms of parties. What I remember with more pleasure are the long, intensely quiet mornings, the games of croquet at the Browns', where we gathered on Sunday afternoon, the weekday afternoons spent fishing by myself or walking in the woods with Hart, and the talks about poets and poetry. Hart had a purely unselfish project that summer: he was going to prod me into collecting a book of poems. "I have it at least in mind," he wrote to Isidor and Helen Schneider in July, "to try my best to get his poems accepted by some publisher or other before a twelvemonth. He'll never do much about it himself, as you know, and his collection is really needed on the shelves these days."

Hart was right in thinking that I would have been very slow to do anything about it myself. I had sixty-odd poems, all printed in magazines during the preceding ten years — there was an immediacy that I enjoyed in magazine publication — but I felt no urgent desire to make a book of them. Although the book might come in time, I rather preferred to be unknown for the moment — except to magazine readers — and therefore unclassified and free to move in any direction. But Hart kept prodding me. Early in July he made me assemble a sheaf of poems; then we went over them together, rejecting some by mutual consent and discussing which of the others belonged together, and in exactly what order. Hart believed that emotions, and the poems that expressed them, should follow one another in the right sequence. He thought naturally in terms of structure and of "the book," which, he insisted, should be more than a random selection of poems by one author. In the poems themselves he did not change a word — not even later, when he retyped the whole manuscript — since both of us felt that a poet should speak in his own voice. He did point out some lines, not more than two or three, that he thought were weaker than others, and I must have revised them — but then I was always revising. Once he suggested that, for greater emphasis, I should change the order of words in a line. The rearrangement would have put a relative pronoun before its antecedent, as in Hart's own line, "And afterwards, who had a colt's eyes — one said." Enjoying that line as I did, I was still determined not to copy it. The word order I tried to follow in my verse was that of good English prose, a habit that may have been part of what Hart liked to call my "genial pedestrianism."

When he left for New York City early in August, there was a book of sorts, one that might have been printed, but still I had only a vague notion of showing it to a publisher. Hart's notion was much more definite. On October 24 he asked me — it wasn't the first time, for some of his letters have been lost — "to bring in all the mss material of your poems which I was in the process of editing last summer. I'll soon have plenty of time to give the matter, and I have a suspicion that something will come of it now." On November 20 he announced in a drunken early-morning letter that the poems had arrived the day before. "I'll be careful with the mss," he wrote. "And your book'll be out within 7 months," that is, within the "twelvemonth" he had mentioned in his letter to the Schneiders. On December 1, a week before sailing for Europe, he wrote, "It has been a pleasure for me to spend part of the last two days in typing the mss of your book. . . . I now have two copies, one to turn over to the 'secret' arbiter here and one to take with me to England." He had omitted one poem that both of us had questions about and had changed the position in the manuscript of three others. "Really the book as we now have it," he said, "has astonishing structural sequence," thus ending the sentence with two of his favorite words. The original manuscript was being returned to me by registered mail.

A few weeks later, when Hart was in London or Paris, I heard from the "secret arbiter." He turned out to be Gorham Munson, then an editor at the George H. Doran Company, which later merged with Doubleday. Munson and I had been on opposite sides of the quarrels in 1923 that preceded the death of *Broom* and *Secession;* of course that was why Hart hadn't mentioned his name. Now Munson laid the quarrels aside. In the name of his company he offered me a contract for the book — it had by then acquired a title, *Blue Juniata* — together with a modest advance against royalties. Hart's project was bearing fruit, and in less than the "twelve-month" he had specified.

At this point, however, the project was interrupted by the stiff-necked character of the author. Grateful as I was to Hart, I had a Pennsylvania Dutch side that hated to be — as my forebears would have said — "beholden" to anyone for the structure and publication of my first book. I thanked Munson for the offer and said that I would think about it. Then I showed the original manuscript to Harrison Smith, a friend of mine (and of Hart's) who had started a publishing house in partnership with Jonathan Cape of London. Hal, as everyone called him, promptly accepted it and gave me a slightly larger advance than Doran had offered.

I took the manuscript home — we were spending the winter in a cramped apartment on Avenue B, south of the present East Village — and set to work on it. First I gave it a completely different sequence, not emotional, as Hart had suggested, but autobiographical. The new framework made it possible to use a few of the poems that Hart and I had earlier decided to omit. These were callow, as we had agreed, but their callowness was part of the story I was telling. Then I divided the book into five sections and furnished notes, in prose, to introduce three of them. Finally I revised most of the poems once more, a task that continued through the winter, though it was interrupted when I had to do translations to pay the rent. Meanwhile Hart had carried his copy of the original manuscript to Paris and was trying to persuade Harry Crosby to publish it at the Black Sun Press. He was on the point of succeeding when I wrote to him late in January that the book was coming out in New York.

By the middle of June *Blue Juniata* was in type, and I sent an extra set of galleys to Hart. I was a little afraid that his vanity would be wounded by my failure to accept his suggestions, but I need not have been, for Hart had almost no vanity of the sort. He was not interested in whether the book embodied his ideas, but only in whether it was put together effectively. "Since reading the proofs," he wrote me on July 3, 1929, "I'm certain that the book is even better ... a much more solidified unit than it was before. I haven't had the original mss with me for comparison, but wherever I have noted changes they seem to be for the better. Nor do I regret any of the additions. I like the added bulk of the book. Really, Malcolm — if you will excuse me for the egoism — I'm just a little proud at the outcome of my agitations last summer." It had been exactly twelve months since he started them.

As I piece together the story now, with a renewed feeling of gratitude to Hart, I think again how different he was in spirit from the drunken rioter he is often pictured as being. All this took place in the period of his noisiest riots, and yet he devoted sober weeks to editing and typing and peddling the manuscript of a friend. He was absolutely lacking in professional jealousy, except toward T. S. Eliot, and that was a compliment to Eliot; otherwise Hart was jealous only of the great dead. The little victories gained by his friends delighted him more than his own victories. "You're a lucky boy!" he wrote to me after reading some favorable reviews of *Blue Juniata*. "I'm very glad about it all" — and he truly was. He was the first person to whom I sent an inscribed copy of the book. "If it's bad," I wrote on the flyleaf, "the sin be on your head." He carried the book to Mexico and still had it with him when he sailed home on the *Orizaba*. Peggy Cowley retrieved it from his stateroom the day after he died.

M. C.

While this was going on: In the fall of 1928, both Bill and I had to take jobs in New York; there was a baby to be supported. Through Matty Josephson's recommendation, I was engaged as book editor by the Macaulay Publishing Company, for which Bill was translating from the French. The Josephsons also found us an apartment on a lower floor of the building in which they lived, on East Twelfth Street between Third and Second Avenues in Manhattan, so, without knowing it, we became the first "East Villagers." In turn, we located the Bovings in a large apartment a few doors down the block from us, so that Johanne could be close to her beloved "Gwiffy," then nine months old. (A year later, in October of 1929, Malcolm was made an editor of *The New Republic* and Bill was soon engaged as an editorial assistant there). One of my first jobs at Macaulay was to see through the press the second *American Caravan,* in which Hart's poem "The River" appeared. Lewis Mumford and Paul Rosenfeld, as initiators and editors of the *American Caravan* series, came to the Macaulay office frequently, and I enjoyed working with them. They had scrupulous respect for their authors' wishes as to the styling and printing of their copy. Mine was the modest but exacting task of preparing the copy for the printer, in accordance with the editors' policies, and reading the proofs. Variation in the style of punctuation was a copy-editing headache in this collection of about one hundred highly individualistic writers. E. E. Cummings and others had launched a revolution against standard punctuation. By 1928 a number of writers would have nothing to do with inverted commas, single or double, around quoted speech. Usually Hart's copy-styling was in accord with standard usage, but it happened that his typed copy of "The River" did not use quotation marks. There was some discussion as to whether quotes would help to emphasize that it was a convict on a road gang, not the poet, who recalled his Aunt Sally's Louisiana smile. The *Caravan* editors abided by the poet's styling. Later on, when "The River" was set up for *The Bridge,* the poet himself decided to employ quotes, which have been retained in subsequent editions.

From this period, two written relics of Hart survive in the Browns' papers. One is a short note addressed to "Bill," implying a current literary or publishing controversy:

"Here's the clipping from the *Herald Tribune.* On further consideration I don't think it's serious enough to bother about — just too terrible to be answered. But people like Isabel Paterson certainly do know how to be thoroughly offensive. I shall ring you for lunch soon."

So "I.M.P." of the "Turns with a Bookworm" column was spared.

The second written relic from this period is in a different vein. Hart's reference to "ringing you for lunch soon" recalls a feature of those days that had been initiated by Kenneth Burke during Hart's stay in California, and had been continued: the custom of meeting for lunch once a week by half a dozen or so literary-minded young men, the nucleus being Kenneth, Malcolm, Bill Brown, Isidor Schneider, Matty Josephson, and visiting friends from The Hub and Montparnasse. Hart came frequently during his Henry L. Doherty days, when he worked near the Armenian restaurant on Washington Street in the lower reaches of Manhattan in which the group sometimes met. On one occasion, when both Bill and Hart were present, the discussion turned to the non-literary subject of methods of interment. Hart expressed vehement distaste for earthen burial, with, as he kept reiterating, its connotation of "the worms crawl out, and the worms crawl in." He plumped for cremation as his personal choice, though he avoided that word. Bill told him he would have to leave explicit instructions for cremation, so Hart asked Bill to write down to his dictation and then witness his wording of his "explicit instructions," Bill pulled out his small pocket notebook and wrote on a blank page the following last will and testament to Hart's dictation:

> I, Hart Crane, under my right mind and full sensibilities, hereby insist and do declare that it is my wish and devout demand that upon the occasion of my demise into the hands of our Lord of Eternity and the Great Hereafter — that my mortal remains shall be committed to the flames.
>
> Harold Hart Crane
>
> (Witness):
> Wm. Slater Brown

Hart made frequent trips from Brooklyn Heights to East Twelfth Street — to dance, to drink, to complain about his mother, to play my old records from the Jones Street days of 1923 and 1924, and my new Marlene Dietrich records in German. He was *mad* about her voice in *"Ich bin von Kopf bis Fusz auf Liebe eingestellt,"* as I was, and would play it far beyound Bill's, and even my, endurance. Among the old Jones Street records, our favorites were a Ted Lewis version of "Saint Louis Blues," a "Farewell Blues," a "Stack O'Lee Blues" ("Stackerlee" in some versions), "Some Sunny Day," "Melinda's Wedding Day," and a vocal from the musical comedy *Poppy* entitled "What Do You Do Sunday, Mary?"

Devotees of popular music will find traces of these songs and others scattered through Hart's poetry. He already knew some of them back in Cleveland; hearing them again on Jones Street would set him off on a nostalgic binge. I find reminders of the rhythms, and some verbal evocations, of these pop songs especially in Part II of "Faustus and Helen." He acknowledges this in the line: "Let us take her on the incandescent wax . . ." "Melinda's Wedding Day" (1913) emerges in:

Rhythmic ellipses lead into canters
Until somewhere a rooster banters —

— which prompts in me a desire to sing it to the tune of:

"What's dat? What's dat?
Ain't dat a rooster crowin'?"

from "Melinda." He mentioned "Some Sunny Day" in
"The River" in the roster of songs that he heard a road-gang
chanting. These effects were deliberately aimed at. He
wrote to Allen Tate on May 16, 1922:

". . . but one *does* have joys. The vocabulary of damna-
tions and prostrations has been developed at the expense of
these other moods, however, so that it is hard to dance in
the proper measure." Then, farther on: "Let us invent an
idiom for the proper transposition of jazz into words! Something clean, sparkling, elusive!"

Perhaps Hart's most demonstrable conversion of pop
lyrics and rhythms into the words and rhythms of poetry is in the song "Virginia," in Section V of *The Bridge,*
which has more than hints of "What Do You Do Sunday,
Mary?" After *The Bridge* was published, I mentioned this
parallel to Hart; he was pleased to have me spot it and
readily acknowledged it. Irving Caesar's words in the song
are:

What do you do Sunday,
What do you do Monday,
　　Ma — ry?
What do you do Tuesday,
What do you do Wednesday,
　　Ma — ry?
When ere I call you're hardly ever alone;
You always have some other plan of your own.

What do you do Thursday,
What do you do Friday,
　　Ma — ry?

Where did you get *this* from?
Where did you get *that* from,
    Ma — ry?
It's only Saturday that you can be found.
What do you do, Ma — ry, all — week — 'round?

The pertinent lines from "Virginia" are:

O rain at seven
Pay-check at eleven —
Keep smiling the boss away,
Mary (what are you going to do?)
Gone seven — gone eleven,
And I'm still waiting you —
O Blue-eyed Mary with the claret scarf,
    Saturday Mary, mine! . . .
O Mary, leaning from the high wheat tower,
    Let down your golden hair! . . .
Out of the way-up nickel-dime tower shine,
      Cathedral Mary,
        Shine!

Hart's five-and-ten virgin is more virtuous than Irving
Caesar's, who is not above accepting a present or so, though
she *may* "keep smiling her boss away." Hart's use of the
Rapunzel theme here is obvious and has been mentioned.
Perhaps not so obvious is his use of other sources that make
this seemingly slight song so rich: that, in the Roman Catholic canon, Saturday is the day of the Virgin Mary; that the
pseudo-Gothic Woolworth Building on Lower Broadway
with its "way-up nickel-dime tower" was commonly referred to, in its early days, as the "Five and Ten Cathedral"; and that when the setting sun turned its glassy tower
gold, from a ferry boat in the river a poetic imagination
could see a little Five-and-Ten salesgirl-virgin letting down
her golden hair from her Cathedral tower — but only for
her true suitor on her free Saturday.

Letter #27.   To WSB. From RMS *Rumrunia,* off the coast of Ireland.   Near Christmas of 1928.

Dear Bill:

The trip has been one song and dance practically all the way. Rum — which wasn't even priced on the wine list — is now the favorite with the quarter deck and high cabin folks as well as the foc'sle — where, as you might imagine, I've paid my respects.

I seem to be the only American in this cabin and enjoy the distinction. In explaining away the faults of my countrymen I seem to have entered the bosoms of some very pleasant people. If they're at all typical I'm in for "happy days" as they say when the ale is lifted.

The air is like April today — in fact the trip has been extraordinarily placid for this season of the year.

Some of the people on board you'd love — Mr. Pickwick, actually, to say nothing of Falstaff and Mrs. Gamp and a whole gallery of half-Irish and Australian novelties.

At the masque ball two nights ago I made more than an impression as the sergeant-major. Flaming red coat, sailor hat, dress breeches — all lined with rum and brandy! Well — you know the rest —

I would enjoy another week of the sea — but probably won't feel that way tomorrow after Havre. That and Plymouth are the two ports yet before London.   Love,   Hart

Letter #28.   To MC. From Paris.   February 4, 1929

Dear Malcolm:

Time here flies faster than I can count. And now along comes the good news from you about the book of poems. Of course I'm all the happier that you got better terms from Hal — it's all to the good. But I do hope that you have seen Munson by this time and at least thanked him for his interest. For the very fact that you were able to make such an announcement to Hal may well have influenced his interest to a great extent. Such matters are rather officious for me to mention, I fear, but I do feel that Munson deserves some real credit.

I'm sorry to hear that Peggy has been so afflicted. I came the nearest ever to flu in London and really have been tagging around with a bit of it ever since.

I'm dizzy, also, with meeting people. "Teas" are all cocktails here — and then that's just the start of the evening. And as lions come these days, I'm known already, I fear, as the best "roarer" in Paris.

Have just returned from a weekend at Ermenonville (near Chantilly) on the estate of the Duc de La Rochefoucauld where an amazing millionaire by the name of Harry Crosby has fixed up an old mill (with stables and a stockade all about) and such a crowd as attended *is* remarkable. I'm invited to return at any time for any period to finish the Bridge, but I've an idea that I shall soon wear off my novelty. Anyway, Crosby who inherited the famous Walter Berry (London) library has such things as first editions of Hakklyt (I can't spell today) and is going to bring out a private edition of the Bridge with such details as a reproduction of Stella's picture in actual color as frontispiece. He's also doing Lawrence, Cummings and Kay Boyle. It takes a book to describe the Crosbys — and it has (I mean the connection) already led me to new atrocities — such as getting drunk yesterday and making violent love to nobility. As le comte was just about to marry, I couldn't do better, though all agree (including Kay Boyle and Lawrence Vail) that I did my best. Those last named, by the way, are consuming each other in Hymen's flames, these days.

I'm supposed to be off for a short trip to Villefranche, Toulouse and Marseilles this week — but keep on writing me here. I'm not going to Mallorca — want to learn French and stay here.

Best love to Peggy   and write soon & often.

Hart

Tell Lorna I'll write her soon.

Letter #29. To WSB. From Collioure, France. 25
            Avril, 1929

Bill:

Why the hell don't you write to me? You used to. And here I am, sitting by the shore of the most shockingly beautiful fishing village — with towers, baronial, on the peaks of the Pyrenees all about, wishing more than anything else that you were on the other side of the table.

This begins to look as good as the West Indies. Maybe — if I could talk Catalan it would be better. I begin to feel as you predicted about Paris. Wish you were with me! I don't know whether you want to hear from me or not — since you have never written — but here's my love anyway, Bill —

Letter #30. To MC. From Paris. July 3, 1929

Dear Malcolm:

Since reading the proofs I'm certain that the book is even better than before. And the notes! — When you first mentioned them to me I admit having trembled slightly at the idea. But since seeing them I haven't a doubt. The maturity of your viewpoint is evident in every word. Humour and sincerity blend into some of the cleverest and most adroit writing I know of, leaving the book a much more solidified unit than it was before. I haven't had the original mss. with me for comparison, but wherever I have noted changes they seem to be for the better. Nor do I regret any of the additions. I like the added bulk of the book. Really, Malcolm — if you will excuse me for the egoism — I'm just a little proud at the outcome of my agitations last summer. "Blue Juniata" will have a considerable sale for a long period to come, for the bulk of it has a classical quality — both as regards material and treatment — that won't suffer rejection by anyone who cares or who will later care for American letters.

I would particularize more copiously except that I'm expecting to see you within relatively so short a time.

I'll be back in NY by the first of September at the latest, and I may be back a month before. Perhaps it's just as well that a good part of my money is tied up in a savings account in New York and inaccessible to me here. As it is, I haven't any great regrets about coming back at this time. When I come to France again I'll sail direct for Marseille — and it's certainly my intention to come again! I'm looking forward to talking it all over with you — so get a little cider ready for the occasion!

The Crosbys are bringing out the Bridge in December or January — that is, it'll be finished and on sale by that time. Yes, you can have a copy — but don't tell anyone about it. I don't get very many gratis — and I might like to sell a half dozen of them myself. Why not? Certainly that wouldn't be any more ignoble than the McSorley book-raid which you played such a friendly part in. I certainly *am* grateful!

I wish Vanity Fair could have something better than they likely got from the Isle of Pines period. But they'll probably have too good taste to use any of those anyhow — and anyway, I can't imagine a much greater absurdity than putting me, at this early date, in any of their public albums!

S'much for now, and as Jack Fitzin used to say — "it won't be long now." ...

As ever, — Hart

Comment: During the four months preceding *Letter #29* from Collioure, we had received occasional notes and post cards from Hart, and, at greater length, distressing news from friends in France about Hart's intoxication in public, sometimes resulting in drunken brawls. This news put a damper on our response to his notes and post cards. His increasing inability to tolerate alcohol, observed during his last months in New York, had made the most sanguine of his friends apprehensive as to what might happen away from his home base.

His close friends at home had tried to restrain his conduct, with some success. It may be remembered that in November of 1923, Hart had written to me: "All advice from you is good. Too damned sensible, as you have heard me complain." The sequence of letters to Malcolm in the fall of 1928 were not written — could not have been written — by a constant inebriate. Even during this Paris "wild life," as he himself called it, he had made progress on preparing *The Bridge* for publication by the Black Sun Press in Paris, operated by Harry and Caresse Crosby.

The Crosbys had taken Hart up in a big way; he was a frequent guest at house-parties in their remodeled "mill" at Ermenonville. Lawrence Vail, also a frequent Crosby guest, had written me: "Your friend Hart Crane is a great success here." And then, either quoting or initiating, I don't know which, he had added: *"C'est pas un homme — c'est un ouragan."* Hart's admission to Malcolm was: "As lions come these days, I'm known already, I fear, as the best 'roarer' in Paris." He had hoped that his solitary life in Collioure would help him to recuperate while he prepared the finished section of *The Bridge* for the press and worked on unfinished parts; he did not add to it to any extent, however, until his return to the United States. His stay of three weeks at Collioure had been a failure. He was lonely and homesick there: "I wish you were with me! I don't know whether or not you want to hear from me —" He wrote Isidor Schneider that he kept "thinking of my room out there in Patterson" — Mrs. Turner's. So, he left Collioure and spent most of May and all of June in and near Marseille, indulging in more of the same "wild life." Then back to Paris to confer with the Crosbys and turn over what work he had done on *The Bridge*.

A day or so after his good letter to Malcolm, on July 3, 1929, he got into the worst brawl of all, the cause of his precipitate return to New York. It came about through his quarrel with a café waiter who refused to let him sign for drinks when he found himself without cash. Americans present offered to pay, but the waiter and the management refused, summoned gendarmes, and Hart, still battling, was dragged along the street to the police station and from there thrown into a cell at La Santé. It took a week for Harry Crosby and other friends to gain his release. This incident was reported in the Paris *Herald Tribune* and picked up in the New York press. Hart hastily wound up his affairs in Paris and, supplied with cash by Crosby, sailed for New York, late in July of 1929, without having notified his friends there.

Bill and I were working in New York that summer, spending only week-ends and vacations at Robber Rocks. During the heat of July and August our little boy "Gwiffy," then a walking tot, was boarded with Agnes O'Neill's mother who lived in Agnes's farmhouse in nearby Merryall Valley, where we picked him up each week end and took him home to Robber Rocks. On an airless, hot day that summer I came home from work and found Hart in our Twelfth Street flat, brought there by Bill, who had run into him wandering morosely around by himself. Bill was always meeting people on the street. Hart had been in New York for some days, keeping to himself, he said. His eight months' absence had made a change in his appearance: complexion red and somewhat mottled, hair grayer, figure slightly puffy — this at twenty-nine. When I greeted him affectionately and scolded him for not looking us up immediately, he embraced me and tears came to his eyes. "I thought you would never want to see me again," he murmured — again the thought that had bothered him in Collioure, in his letter to Bill. Shame and regret for misbehavior and concern for what the persons he cared for thought of him could hardly have been more evident.

But he had remarkable recuperative powers, and was soon himself again. He still had a sizable portion of his inheritance, left behind in a bank, and was thus able to rent a modest furnished apartment at 130 Columbia Heights. He also re-established relations with Mrs. Turner and resumed occupancy of his rooms in Pawling, which he had retained during his absence. He worked steadily on revising and adding to *The Bridge*, as he had promised Crosby he would do, while writing the Crosbys excellent detailed suggestions for the format and typography. Most of the interesting marginal glosses appear to have been written during this period. He was in and out of the city, seeing about the regular trade edition by Liveright and carrying out other chores for the Black Sun Press edition.

Malcolm's *Blue Juniata* was issued at this time, and was being reviewed, as the following letter to Malcolm shows.

Letter #31. To MC. From 130 Columbia Heights,
August 22, 1929
Dear Malcolm:

You're a lucky boy! I've been reading some beautiful reviews of *Juniata* — especially Allen's in the *New Republic* — and then Kenneth's in the H. Tribune and the Nation, and even Seaver's in the Eve. Post for last Saturday. I'm very glad about it all.

When you and Peggy come in look me up in my new apartment as numbered above. There's no phone yet. But plenty of Mariners! — and whisky, too —

Love, Hart

Comment: Harry and Caresse Crosby arrived in New York early in December of 1929, bringing advance proofs of the Black Sun edition of *The Bridge.* With the help of a few women friends, Hart gave a large party for them in his Columbia Heights apartment — the only party that he ever gave, to my knowledge, beyond serving tea from his beloved Canton china, to two or three country neighbors in his rooms at Mrs. Turner's. He was in high spirits, delighted to have a host of his old friends around him, while his new friends, the Crosbys, circulated sample pages of the handsomely designed *Bridge.* For the past few months, since his return, he had been working fairly steadily, with no prolonged binges. Here were the printed pages to show for it.

He had recovered his self-respect. So he made a genial host, danced with all the ladies, saw to it that the Crosbys had a good time and met everybody, and, in spite of the flowing bowl, kept himself in good shape to the end.

Though the party was a success, some of us had noticed a disturbing undertone, for which Hart was not responsible. I went home feeling uneasy about it. A few days later Crosby's suicide in spectacular circumstances made headlines because of the prominence and wealth of his family. By chance the unwelcome task of giving this news to Crosby's wife and mother fell to Hart.

Nevertheless, a few days later Caresse Crosby returned to France at her scheduled time, taking with her the corrected proofs of *The Bridge*. Copies of the impressive Black Sun Press edition arrived in New York in February, with the regular trade edition due from Liveright in March. These concerns kept Hart occupied for the most part. He was in fairly good shape, mentally and physically, when he gave up his Columbia Heights apartment and settled in at Mrs. Turner's, still feeling the sad and sobering effects of Crosby's suicide.

During April, May, and June he was busy corresponding with reviewers, critics and admiring friends and working on an elaboration of the statement of intentions for *The Bridge* that he had sent to Otto Kahn several years earlier. One of the editors of the *American Caravan*, Paul Rosenfeld, had asked Hart's permission to publish it in the edition in progress at that time. All told, these three months in the country were a "good old Hart" period.

One incident suggests the tone of our neighborhood life at that time, one in which I did not participate, for I was at my job in New York. When I went up to Robber Rocks for the week-end, I was told about it in detail. It was cherry-picking time, and a number of neighbors had gathered to pick and can the large, dark-red cherries from the mammoth old cherry tree on our front lawn. Present were Fitzi (a countrywoman born on a Wisconsin farm, she was always an ardent canner); a delegation from the Bovings;

Bina and Romolo; and a scattering of the Porwitzkis, in addition to Bill. Fitzi and the Porwitzki girls were in charge in the kitchen, canning as fast as the cherries were picked and sorted by the men. Hart came to pick some cherries for his lunch, then went back home along the wood path. The adults were all so intent on the cherries that little Gwiffy was left to play with Pearl, the Porwitzkis' dog. When Pearl wandered off along the path Hart had taken, Gwiffy followed her. Back in his room half a mile away, Hart heard the childish voice talking to Pearl, and expected to hear Bill's greeting, which didn't come. Looking out the window he saw Gwiffy and Pearl well on their way to the Akins' dairy farm, another half mile ahead, so he pursued them and carried the boy back to the cherry pickers on his shoulders, both of them in high spirits. He found only an agitated Fitzi at Robber Rocks, for the cherry pickers had sent out posses in several directions, alarmed because of the pitfalls in the woods. One posse had already returned disconsolate from the wood path and gone elsewhere. The relieved Fitzi summoned the searchers back on a Tally-ho horn, as had been planned. Hart was the hero of the day.

By mid-July financial worries and the proximity of a congenial bootlegger proved too much for him — this, at least, is my opinion, for I saw no evidence that he was unduly disturbed by critical responses to *The Bridge,* as some critics have written. Yvor Winters' "reversal of opinion," as he called it, Hart took with humor: "Poets should defer alluding to the sea, also, I presume, until Mr. Winters has got an invitation for a cruise." One evening he returned to Addie's after a long session at the bootlegger's, unsteady on his feet, which was rare with him, and rambling about the house carrying a smoking kerosene lamp. Her protests were ignored, and, her patience tried beyond endurance, she ordered him to leave. In a rage, Hart immediately ran the mile and a half to Fitzi's. Always kind-hearted, Fitzi got him to bed and told him he could stay at her house for the time being. The next day Eva and June-oh!, with Walter Adams' wagon, helped him move his belongings from Mrs.

Turner's, dividing them between Fitzi's house and Robber Rocks. The trustful Fitzi left him in charge of her dog, and went back to her job. He had lost the home he had cherished since 1925.

After hanging his pictures and arranging his belongings neatly in Fitzi's orderly house, he went off for a short visit to the Cummingses in New Hampshire, with Lorna Dietz as a companion. His main interest for the rest of the summer was a close reading of Dante, inspired by T. S. Eliot's essay. Late in August, still at Fitzi's, he sent off an application for a Guggenheim fellowship, then went to New York to seek work. He looked up Russell Davenport of *Fortune*, who started him off on two jobs. One was to write a profile of Standard Oil's Walter Teagle; the other was to write an article about the George Washington Bridge, then nearing completion over the Hudson. His pleased father, a friend of Teagle's, sent him an introduction to the great man, and Hart interviewed him. "I managed to keep the oil king talking far beyond the time allotted," he wrote a Cleveland friend, "but when I come to write it up in typical *Fortune* style the jams gather by the hundred." The "Bridge" assignment was more to his taste, at first. His recital of his uneasy progress along a high catwalk in a high wind raised the hair on the heads of his friends as the experience itself had done to him. He turned in articles to Davenport, declaring his own dissatisfaction with them. *Fortune* agreed.

In the face of increasing national mass unemployment, this failure left him no alternative but to accept his father's suggestion that he help out in the Crane candy stores in Cleveland and in Crane's Canary Cottage in Chagrin Falls during the pre-Christmas business. Hart was later to mention that the sight of the bread and soup lines everywhere in New York City had decided him on the Cleveland move. In December he took refuge in Chagrin Falls. Here he spent several months at steady hard labor, in complete but uneasy and sterile sobriety. Early in March he received notice of his appointment as a Guggenheim fellow. The next letter reports his move to Mexico.

An Explanation: I knew the man

I am aware that this account of Hart's behavior during this post-European period — say from August 1929 until December 1930 — is not in accord with much that has been written by others. He is shown here as working fairly steadily and during most of the first twelve months with good results. Today his large correspondence of this period makes good reading. His social life entered new phases. After the publication of *The Bridge* he was welcomed into new circles, where he acquitted himself well, meanwhile keeping up his old intimacies. When the flurry of reviews and correspondence over the two editions of *The Bridge* had slowed up, he made consistent efforts to support himself in the commercial sphere in the face of rising mass unemployment, for the great depression already had a firm grip on the country. For months he worked steadily at the two projects opened up to him by Russell Davenport for *Fortune,* work that was far removed from his natural gifts. Many others with no inclination toward alcohol have tried and failed at similar tasks.

As to the actual occurrence of *most* of the violent acts that have been related: they did indeed occur. The point I wish to make is that these events were few; they occupied a short span of time; they did not add up to a way of life. Yet during the first years after Hart's death they were in the forefront of his friends' minds. We were reviewing mentally the incidents that perhaps we should have recognized as the warning signals of tragedy. Why had we not taken them more seriously? Couldn't we have done something? These were disturbing questions. Philip Horton undoubtedly received a load of such memories several years later, when he began assembling material for his moving biography.

Hart's six months in California had advanced him well along the road toward alcoholism. But I am skeptical as to the sweeping scale of his indulgence, in this pre-Mexican period, especially as to the accuracy of the reports of his night after night sorties, intoxicated, into low dives on Sands Street in Brooklyn — repeatedly being beaten up by sailors and arrested or beaten by police for "solicitation." The very use of this word suggests an unreliable source. There may have been one fracas with a sailor — which is bad enough, as a portent. Horton notes with some surprise that Hart's appearance never did show the symptoms of advanced alcoholism. The reason is that he had not reached that stage. He was still at what Alcoholics Anonymous calls a "high bottom." I saw him frequently during this period. He was always neat, clean, decently dressed and groomed, his usual articulate, affectionate, entertaining self — not often intoxicated. He appears never to have hit what A.A. calls a "low bottom." Alcoholics Anonymous was not organized until 1934. If Hart and his friends could have turned to A.A. for aid in 1930, his fate might well have been different. Much worse cases than he have recovered.

"The Last Days of Hart Crane" by Peggy Baird gives in her dramatic narrative the main events in Hart's life during his last seven months in Mexico, when she was with him much of the time. His inauspicious start on this life has been described by the noted bacteriologist, the late Dr. Hans Zinsser, in his autobiography, *As I Knew Him* (1940). Dr. Zinsser was on the same ship on the way to Mexico, the *Orizaba* (under a Captain Blackadder, as he reports). He became friendly with Hart and spent much time with him. Though Hart put him and his assistant through one difficult evening, he remained attached to him, continued to see him in Mexico, and, as Philip Horton puts it, "developed a fatherly concern for him." Hart's prose poem "Havana Rose," written as soon as he was settled in Mixcoac, gives his "humble, fond remembrances of the great bacteriologist."

*Letter #32.   To WSB.   On Board S.S. Orizaba.   April 6,
        1931.*
Dear Bill:
        I have several hours in Havana tomorrow — and two more days on the Gulfo. It's a nice trip, and I'm gradually "piping down" after the rush and intensity of the last few days in NY.

I didn't see half enough of you — nor of Sue — and now you've got to make amends by dropping me word occasionally. Also, I hope it won't trouble you too much to have the address of your gift (N.R.) changed from Chagrin Falls to

c/o Dr. Eyler N. Simpson
Apartado 538
Mexico, D.F.

He's the Guggenheim official representative in those parts, and Moe told me that he'd take more than a banking interest in my mail, etc.

So — Heigh-ho and Yo-ho, caro hermano! There's good rum on board, and the Captain is very much a Dane! But I'm not depending too much on either.

Yrs always, and much, much love to Sue — Hart

Comment: Hart's "piping down" did not occur. His first months in Mexico were marred by several incidents, when intoxicated, that involved him in trouble. The worst was with Katherine Anne Porter who, after having him as a guest, had found him a house in Mixcoac near that in which she and her husband were then living. From this time on, there are signs that Hart began to realize he had a serious alcohol problem. Instead of facing it, he tried to conceal his worst misdeeds from his friends, and to minimize his offenses. — The gift Hart refers to was a subscription to the *New Republic.* — Henry Allen Moe headed the Guggenheim Foundation. He later bought the Charlie Jennings' house in Sherman, a mile from Robber Rocks.

Letter #33. To MC. From Mexico. June 2, 1931
Michoacan 15,
Mixcoac, DF

Dear Malcolm:

Look up Bill Spratling, whom I saw off a week ago for NY. He's staying at 603 Park Ave. for a coupla weeks; then intends (or *intended*) to cruise back to his Taxco. Meanwhile I'm trying to take care of all his precious collection of timeless, or rather dateless, idols.

An even more "advance notice" concerns the early arrival (permanent) of Malu Cabrera, the nicest and most interesting woman in Mexico, who is coming up within three weeks or so to marry a guy named "Bloch," I think it's his name, who's a reader for Knopf. She hates his crowd, the Van Vechten set, from previous encounters. Let Spratling tell you about her. She is very much somebody — especially in Mexico. Have her around to one of those "ordeal" luncheons at the New Rep. because she'll always know so damned much more about Mexico than anyone else (including little Carleton Beals) who has ever stepped into the doors of your institution, that it'll pay to have her handy for a lot of timely references.

Malu will probably end up in NY by serving conventional enough "teas" — but here in Mexico, being the daughter of a great international corporation lawyer and a real Mexican patriot — (what a combination!) — she's considered more advanced and "independent" in her actions than any señorita who ever left home and "earned her way" in convent and as school teacher. She's a beautiful and agile and strong, direct creature. And you'll miss a lot if you don't take her up — I.E. as far as her husband . . . will let her'nyouboth. Failing due attentions, on your part, to Spratling, — I'll drive her to you with a letter. . . . As I am to the Davenports, Paul Rosenfeld, and some others.

Don't expect much more from me about Mexico for a while. Maybe it's the altitude (which *is* a tremendous strain at times) maybe my favorite drink, Tequila; maybe my balls and the beautiful people; or maybe just the flowers that I'm growing or fostering in my garden . . . but it's all too good, so far, to be true. I've been too preoccupied, so far, with furnishing, from every little nail, griddle, bowl and pillow, to look around much outside the fascinating city markets and streets and bars. No chance to stretch pennies — just to spend them. Ran out long ago on my Guggenheim installment. But a house just can't be lived in without a few

essentials. And the main "standard American" essentials
in Mexico cost like hell.

Lorna will have to relay to you the more complete details of my house, should such matters interest you. I found,
by advice, that single mozos weren't apt to be much good.
Pulque sprees three times a day, and the evenings never certain. Besides I needed a woman to cook. Consequently I
have a delightful hide and seek combination — of both func-
tions (page Mormon be sneezed BUnson) besides a new installation of electric lights with just enough "glim" — not to
say Klim — to be pleasant.

Moisés has been swell to me. His innate Aztec refine-
ment; his quiet daring; his generosity (one should avoid an
et cetera in such exceptional cases!) has made me love him
very much. He was very instrumental in my accidental possession of a real decoration: an ancient silver pony bridle
(bells and all!) from the period of the Conquest, about my
neck in a photo taken by Katherine Anne — you shall soon
see, like it, — believe it, or not!

I have a quilty, besides a guilty conscience! Haven't
yet even written to Waldo, whose letters gave me a wonderful sendoff with certain writers here. But Latin American
manners, I have discovered, are rather baffling. Great dinners are planned, but never come off! If Katherine Anne
couldn't explain it all away with references to certain previous experiences of her own, I'd feel quite crushed. As it is,
I don't mind in the least. Because . . . Mexico has incredibly
fine native painters. (You should see the new Diegos in the
Palace!) But all her pretenders to poesy have just read about
orchids in Baudelaire, apparently. I have my most pleasant
literary moments with an Irish revolutionary, red haired
friend of Liam O'Flaherty, shot (and not missed) seventeen
times in one conflict and another; the most quietly sincere
and appreciative person, in many ways, whom I've ever met.
It's a big regret that he's Dublin bound again after three
years from home, in a few weeks. Ernest O'Malley by
name. And we drink a lot together — look at frescoes — and
agree!

You and Muriel have got to come visit me here before long. I can't dare to think how soon I'll be driven to fight for my little place here — and keep it. But I think I will. And it has an entire guest suite. Not that it's pretentious — anything BUT. *BUT* — it's the first real home I've ever had. And the devotion of my servants, for $8. total fees per month, and the flowers, and the fleas — well, Malcolm, I don't wanna ever leava!

Good night! Love to Muriel! and write me soon!

As ever,

Hart

What's happened to Bill? He never answers my letters!!!

Comment: William Spratling, the author of *Little Mexico* (1931) and another recent book of memoirs centering on his life in Taxco, is well known for his silver work and as a collector of Mexican work in silver. — By the date of this letter Hart had already had an alcoholic explosion with Katherine Anne Porter, for which he had abjectly apologized, though he had only a dim idea of what he had done and said. During the next three weeks he maintained a course of good conduct, as is shown by his long, thoughtful letters to Waldo Frank, Selden Rodman, and Morton Dauwen Zabel, then editor of *Poetry,* who asked him to review an important volume of poetry. K. A.'s continued kindness encouraged him to hope he had weathered it out; his avoidance of the topic in the above letter suggests his hope that the incident had not reached their joint friends, and could be ignored. But a more serious explosion on June 22 could hardly be smoothed over so easily. He appealed to Katherine Anne's good nature, asking for her continued tolerance of him because of the impending arrival in Mexico of Peggy, their mutual friend. Malcolm and Peggy Baird Cowley had separated at the beginning of 1931. Peggy was expected to arrive at the end of June to start procedures for a Mexican divorce. But before Peggy had time to arrive, he was summoned back to Chagrin Falls by the sudden

death of his father. — Moisés Sáenz was a high official of the
then Mexican government. — Muriel Maurer was to become
Mrs. Malcolm Cowley early in 1932. — The Browns were too
busy to write very much or very often, though our affection
for Hart was undiminished. Full daytime jobs and translating in the evenings kept both of us going to earn enough for
city and country homes, baby-doctor, and a series of unsatis-
factory "maids." Bill was involved in various Depression
movements. Everybody who had a job worked harder and
longer for less pay. On my precious free evenings I craved
entertainment. Correspondence with distant friends came
hard.

Letter #34. To WSB. From Chagrin Falls, Ohio. July
15, 1931.
Dear Bill:
    I appreciate your letter a very great deal. Your surmise
is very true: while the results of my visit with my father last
winter make me feel the loss more keenly, there is some con-
solation, at the same time, in having realized his qualities
and affection for me more fully than ever before. I'm glad,
too, that at the time of his death — as well as for some
months before — he had been in a singularly happy mood.
And it might have been very painful had there been any
protracted illness, invalidism, etc. Especially with his pre-
disposition toward constant activity. As it was, I don't think
he had more than a passing flash of recognition of what had
occurred.
    I'm here for a month or so, at least. Mrs. Crane wants
me to be of what help I can during the settlement of the estate, pending continuance of certain branches of the business and possible suspension of others. As she and I have always been great friends it's only natural that I should com-
ply. Her grief has been genuinely severe; she's been really
heroic in facing the burden of so many new responsibilities.
    I'll write you more soon. Meanwhile do let me hear

more details of your recent life. Thanks again for your thoughtful letter, Bill. As ever, Hart
PS — Could you have my subscription address for the New Republic changed to Chagrin Falls again?

Letter #35.   To MC.   From Mexico.   October 5, 1931
                                        15, Michoacan,
                                        Mixcoac, D.F.
Dear Malcolm:

Despite its aero stamp, I'm just today in receipt of your letter. Mail service seems to get a little worse and more doubtful here all the time.

Yes, Peggy must have been pretty close to danger for a while judging by what she said about her symptoms. She stayed in bed for a week or so, but went to Puebla over last weekend and looked very well this morning when I called. I think she's got to keep pretty quiet, however, if relapses aren't to be expected. Bill Spratling wired me to bring her along with me to Taxco tomorrow for a few days, and I think she's planning on joining me since I've had no word to the contrary this afternoon. She was going to ask her doctor about it.

About cashing checks: I haven't made any connections myself yet, having depended on Eyler Simpson (of the Foundation) to cash mine up to the first of this month when my Guggenheim letter of credit became valid again. So I can't be of much help in that way. In Peggy's present quandary I suggest sending her (wiring her) American Ex. money orders. It costs more than postage but it isn't so high as direct through Western Union, and it's worth the little extra to both of you to have more peace of mind. I think I paid only $.75 to send $150. to France recently, and they were certainly prompt and efficient. Wells Fargo may have the same service. They seem to have more business in Mexico.

As Bill has probably told you, the Katherine Anne upset accounted for my more than diffidence about seeing most

129

of our mutual friends when I passed through NY. Sometime
I may say more about it, but I'm sick of the subject just now;
and since Mexico is proving to be so much more pleasant
and absorbing to me during this second sojourn, I don't
want to stir up any more unneighborly dust here in Mixcoac
this evening than matches a pleasant mood.

But I do hope to have an answer from you sometime —
a little longer than this last and more in proportion to the
long letter I wrote you from here months and months ago,
and which hasn't even yet been acknowledged. It's getting
dark and I want to get this off before the post office closes,
so more later. I'm glad to be of any help I can to Peggy, love
her as always, and enjoy her company (and we see quite a lot
of each other) immensely. Old friends are a God-send anywhere! Especially when they're as good sports as Peggy is.
She's pretty fragile, but I think she's happy here, possibly
more so than anywhere else right now.

I miss getting the N.R. — which is still probably being
sent to Chagrin Falls. Could you have it switched back to
Mixcoac?

All best to you and Muriel, besides Bill and Sue.

Hastily,

Hart

AND LORNA!
I enclose a picture of the garden side of my house. Pretty
good for $30. per month.

Comment: Hart returned to Mexico from Chagrin Falls
during the first week in September, 1931; he and Peggy
greeted each other with whoops of joy. — By the date of this
letter, Katherine Anne and her husband had already shaken
the dust of Mixcoac, neighborly or unneighborly, from their
feet and were in Europe. After a visit with them, Peggy had
found her own quarters in Mexico City. — Lorna Dietz had
written to Hart in Chagrin Falls that news of his run-in
with Katherine Anne and her husband had reached her.

Hart could not know that this news had come to her not from K. A. but from others in Mexico. He had dodged the subject in correspondence with those of his friends who knew K. A. well and who would be skeptical as to any lack of kindness, generosity and reasonable tolerance on her part. He could not clearly remember what he had said and done when drunk but he feared the worst and tried to avoid the pain of facing it. Lorna was not a close friend of K. A.'s; in his reply to her he admitted the fracas but minimized the extent of his misbehavior, even implying that he had had provocation: a sorry performance indeed, quite unlike his normal self. He refused to accept blame for interfering with Katherine Anne's work, and asked that there be no further mention of the incident.

Letter #36. To WSB. From Mexico. Late October, 1931

Dear Bill:

Please tell Malcolm that his article on the Munson-Josephson "debate" has delayed my dinner by two hours of sore sides! "Old Nick" (Jamaica) Rum *may* have contributed a little to some pleasant distress but I still owe a debt. I wish I had the two previous articles of the series at hand; can't you get Betty to sort them out and send them to me?

From cock-crow to sunset, here in Mixcoac, my life is extremely jolly. And then beyond. How I wish you and Sue were here sometimes! Guitars and *corridas* galore. Even *I* am learning how to sing! One thing I can't seem to get around to do — and that's the reviews I contracted to do for *Poetry.* Have you seen Putnam's new book of poems, *The Five Seasons?* I've got to "do" that, and it's almost too big a job. "Old Nick" and Nicotine keep me too occupied.

From the   hart

PS — Allen's note on Milton was one of the best things in modern criticism I expect to anticipate.

The setting. — I have been taken to task, mildly, by several persons with differing viewpoints, for not being more expansive, or more explicit, about the "Munson-Josephson debate" in my comments on this episode in *The Southern Review*. It has already been written up so thoroughly and by so many that I was, and am, reluctant to add to this literature, the chief items of which are cited below.*

This "debate," which Hart, aided by Old Nick Jamaica Rum, found so entertaining, refers to an article by Malcolm Cowley in the October 21, 1931, issue of *The New Republic,* of which he was then an editor. It was the third article in a series of five, under the general title of "Exile's Return." It bore the sub-head: "Coffee and Pistols for Two." Hart's date on this letter was "Oct. 22nd," obviously too early even with allowance for the usual post-dating by a few days of a weekly magazine. The "debate" was a duel with fists, or at least arms, between Gorham Munson and Matthew Josephson, staged in a muddy field in Woodstock, New York, in early November of 1923, with one spectator, William Murrell Fisher, an art critic and Munson's host. The Josephsons were guests at the Brown-Nagle farmhouse. After a couple of minutes, Fisher induced the battlers to end the scuffle. He later described it as a draw, though the worst fight he had ever seen. There was more slipping and falling than blows, more mud than blood. The "duel" came about at the insistence of Josephson, who re-

* (1) *Exile's Return,* a literary odyssey of the 1920's, by Malcolm Cowley. New York: Viking Press, 1951. (See pages 178–185.) A revision of the *New Republic* series, which ran from Sept. 13, 1931, to Feb. 10, 1932. An earlier edition was issued by Norton in 1937.

(2) Two articles by Gorham Munson: "The Fledgling Years: 1916–24," in the *Sewanee Review,* Jan.–March, 1932, issue; and "A Comedy of Exiles," in the Autumn, 1968, issue of the *Literary Review.* (Fairleigh Dickinson Univ., Rutherford, N.J.)

(3) *Life among the Surrealistes,* a memoir, by Matthew Josephson. New York: Holt, Rinehart and Winston, 1962.

(4) *The Way It Was,* by Harold Loeb. New York: Criterion Books, 1959.

sented charges against him that Munson had written in a letter presented to a gathering of "Aesthetes" associated with *Broom* and *Secession*.

In *The New Republic* article was Malcolm's mock-heroic ode, which he read at a "commemoration" of the battlefield eight months later. A sample:

> And "Up," cried Munson, "with *Secession!*
> Down *Broom*,"he snarls, and warriors pant
> Each to defend his literary slant.

Letter #36 is the last to us. The cheerful note in this letter sounds forced; the postscript is not in Hart's usual lucid style. We received a few later communications from Mexico — a sprinkling of postcards as he traveled about, a note or so enclosing snapshots, with the frequent refrain, "Why don't you write?" One snapshot, which survives, is of a smiling little dark boy of about ten, sitting on a doorstep holding a small white dog between his knees, with Hart's penned note on the back: "My servants' child — named 'Prospero' — our dog is named 'Palomo' — " He never mentioned to us his attachment to Peggy, when it developed. A kind of shyness, I suppose, which is also evident in his letters to Malcolm. He was less reserved in letters to Loveman and Grunberg, who were not a part of that social circle.

By reading *Letters #37, #38, #39* and others written by Hart during the same period — from December of 1931 to April of 1932 — as a consecutive narration, one gets Hart's version of what is essentially the same story that Peggy Baird tells in her memoir — written purely from memory and without documents at hand many years later. It is a tragic and moving story. It may not be the saddest story ever told, but it is quite sad enough. We follow it as Hart experiences a new burst of life, hope, optimism, enthusiasm, resulting in a renewal of poetic creativity. As difficulties piled up, he tried to hold on to this feeling, but the odds were heavy against him. On the outside, the Crane estate was crumbling away; near at hand were the complications he had introduced into his life. His reliance on alcohol had sapped his strength, and then events took over.

Letter #37. To MC. From Mexico. January 9, 1932
                               15 Michoacan, Mixcoac, DF
Dear Malcolm:

I've just returned Maddow's poems to him with a brief note of appreciation, tempered by some objections to his chaotic structural tendencies, etc. It's hard to say much against a person who has so obviously experienced one's own temper and angle of vision. Furthermore, I suspect that he is no more obscure to me (at his *worst*) than I have been to hundreds of others. But what the hell! I don't pretend to excuse myself for a lot of things. He has power and original vision, though, if he's got the conscience and brains to channel them.

Peggy and I had the pleasantest Christmas and New Years together that I remember for ages. Peggy's usual mixed crowd appeared for the former date; but I stayed long enough to enjoy a week alone with her. Taxco is so extremely beautiful — and the townsfolk still so affable — that whatever one has to say about the Yankee occupation (and that ultimately seals its doom) it's still one of the pleasantest places to be. Peggy has probably written you about encounters with Brett, Bynner, King, et al. Lewd limericks were shouted from the rooftops — your collection being more than ever in demand. A mad crowd, though. I had enough Duff (Brett's new name, or nickname) — preferring, as I do, the nautical variety.

I enjoyed your attack on Munson very much — that is, the initial broadside that appeared in the NR. But having read answers and replies since then in *Contempo,* I've lived to regret those later readings — from both sides of the battle line. Of course it was a great mistake for Munson to have replied at all. No dignity could be saved that way — and in the end it put you, too, into a rather apologetic position. Your advantage rests — not chiefly, but partially — in the fact that you initiated the fracas — and in a journal of vastly greater circulation and weight than that little receptacle on Chapel Hill. Now people are beginning to accuse you of being a successful politician. But I hardly agree with that; I think that greater conquests are necessary for that title, even though Mr. Boyd lay flaccid under the same swipe.

I'm damned tired of Mexico City, and want to sublet my house for the remaining three months and get off into Indian towns and territories for a while. If I'm lucky I may get off within three weeks. Hence, better address me, next letter c/o Eyler Simpson, Apartado 538, Mexico, DF. You owe me more than one full letter, old boy; and this may be my last for quite a while. Best to Bill and Sue and Muriel and Betty.

As ever,

Hart

Comment on Letter #37: Paragraph 1. — A young poet, Ben Maddow, had submitted to *The New Republic* a group of poems that strongly showed Hart's influence as well as signs of an original talent. With Maddow's permission, Malcolm sent them to Hart for his comment.

Paragraph 2. — "Lady Brett" is a chief character in Hemingway's *The Sun Also Rises,* regarded as being based on a real-life Englishwoman, Lady Duff Twysden. In 1932, Duff was married to the American painter Clinton King and was living in Mexico, where the poet Witter Bynner also lived. Hart had either confused the real and fictional names of Hemingway's character or else was juggling them for humor. As to "I had enough duff": Hart had originally typed it lower case; he is punning on the various usages of "duff." One of them is a flour pudding, as in "plum duff," a dessert likely to be found on ships' menus. There is another meaning which makes his pun ribald; it can be found in an unabridged dictionary.

Which reminds me: Hart did not go to college but he had acquired a liberal education by wide reading in the fields of literature, criticism, aesthetics, philosophy, history, exploration, and by the constant use of an unabridged dictionary. His memory was excellent. I think his "ignorance" has been exaggerated by some commentators, perhaps because of his lack of a college diploma. An example: the respected critic, Hyatt Howe Waggoner, has written eloquent praise of Hart Crane's poetry in several books, especially of his "Voyages." He also thinks that Hart was "inadequately educated," thinks he used words without knowing their meaning, and sees "ignorance or confusion or both everywhere in Crane except in his best poetry." But, in *The Heel of Elohim,* he cites a poor example to prove his points. He quotes the following sentence from Hart's essay, "Modern Poetry": "The most typical and valid expression of the American *psychosis* seems to me still to be found in Whitman." Then Professor Waggoner queries: "Did he really consider the American character not simply neurotic but *psychotic?* And if so, how did this fit with his intention of celebrating this character and achievement in *The Bridge?*" He concludes that Hart did not know the meaning of the word. Knowing Hart, I doubted that he would have used it without being certain of its accepted meaning. I looked it up in a 1926 edition of Webster's unabridged dictionary, the one current at the time Hart wrote "Modern Poetry." I found that the first and primary definition of *psychosis* was: "any total consciousness at a given moment." Apply this definition to Hart's use of it. Only as a secondary meaning was listed: *"Med.* — a disease of the mind." Over the years this secondary meaning has become the primary one in all the current dictionaries I have looked at — perhaps because of the pervading influence of psychiatry. — Now back to the text of Letter #37.

Paragraph #3 refers to the follow-up comments on the "Munson-Josephson debate" published in a small magazine, *Contempo,* issued in Chapel Hill, North Carolina, written by Gorham Munson, Slater Brown and Malcolm Cowley.

Letter #38.   To MC and Muriel C.   From Mexico.
February 18, 1932

15, Calle Michoacan,
Febrero 18, 1932

Dear Malcolm and Muriel:

I hope it is no profanation of this sacred paper to offer you my genuine and ultimate thanks for the pillow case; a vehicle which ought to carry me, if not back to old Virginny, at least to certain splendid heights of Old, — and Columbian at that!

Here in this pre-Columbian World, one often wonders how much longer the fat will fry or the indians resist a wholesale and picturesque slaughter. It is all this typewriter can do to resist a rape of the tutelary Virgin. I never wrote on such rosy paper before but while it lasts it's yours.

And by the good and generous goodbye, how is Waldo, since all the trucks broke down and bird-shot was welcomed by all? Or was it buckshot? I'm still ignorant about guns, despite my sojourn in this gun toting peninsula. But, as you see I write ornamental letters. And How!

Bill Spratling is dizzy about finally seeing his book in print. Paca Toor and Anita Brenner continue their old feuds. Glad I'm not trying to get my teeth into Mexico — and pull *another* way. My best — and thanks — to you both. I'm here in Mixcoac for some time yet, I conjecture, reckon — and fear. But I'll be sorry to leave, after all.

Affectionately — Hart

Comment on Letter #38: This letter was typed on fancy rose-colored note paper, the words carefully placed around an image of the Virgin of Guadalupe in the center of the sheet. — Waldo Frank, broken-down trucks, gun shots, etc.: this refers to an expedition to Bell County, Kentucky, by a group of American writers led by Waldo Frank and including Edmund Wilson, Malcolm Cowley and Quincy Howe. Their aim was to bring relief to striking coal miners and their families, nearing starvation, and to attract attention to their plight.

Letter #39.   To MC.   From Mixcoac.   March 27, 1932

Easter '32

Dear Malcolm:

Peggy and I think and talk a great deal about you. That means in a very fond way, or it wouldn't be mentioned. I'm wondering whether or not you'll like the above poem — about the first I've written in two years. I'm getting too damned self-critical to write at all any more. More than ever, however, do I implore your honest appraisal of this verse, prose or nonsense — whatever it may seem. Please let me know.

And because I congratulate you most vehemently on your recent account of the Kentucky expedition — please don't tell me anything you don't honestly mean. This has already been submitted to POETRY — so don't worry about that angle.

I miss seeing you a great deal. Peggy is writing you some sort of account of the Easter celebrations here. We're very happy together — and send you lots of love!

Affectionately — Hart

Comment: Malcolm Cowley has written below *Letter #39* this brief note: "This letter was typed at the foot of a manuscript of 'The Broken Tower.' By arrangement with the editors of *Poetry,* the poem was printed in *The New Republic* after Crane's death." The second paragraph refers to Malcolm's article, "Kentucky Coal Town," in the March 2, 1932, issue of *The New Republic,* in which Malcolm relates the experiences of the fifty or so persons who had taken part in the Kentucky expedition early in February. The group were arrested and forbidden to talk to the miners, though they had managed to distribute three truckloads of food, and then were driven out of Kentucky to the Tennessee line. Waldo Frank was severely beaten up in the process. The episode made news. Hart was interested especially because of the participation of Waldo Frank and Malcolm, his close friends. He was also struck by this evidence of the depression-stimulated radicalization of his friends in "The States."

Death by Water: A Reconstruction.

Hart's return to Mexico early in September of 1931 was made under more favorable auspices than his arrival there the preceding April. This time he had his own attractive and comfortable house in Mixcoac. He had just spent two months of sobriety, living in warm friendship with his stepmother, whom he called "Bess." She had showed great generosity and consideration for him, perhaps greater than he realized. Mrs. Crane was a good businesswoman and probably had a much clearer idea than Hart — who seemed to have little or none — of what could be expected from Clarence Crane's estate. Bess had made him feel that he had a home at Crane's Canary Cottage whenever he needed one. Moreover, with her sympathy and approval, his father's will had given him more than a fair share of the estate: $2000 a year in income for four years and after that an equal division with Bess. His mother, Grace Hart Crane, seems to have faded from his mind; at this time she was living unhappily as a hostess in a hotel in Oak Park, Illinois. The estate still had to be probated, but knowing little about the complications of settlement, Hart was obviously optimistic.

Why, then, on passing through New York on his way back to Mexico, was he compelled to abandon himself to alcohol?

There were two related and deeply troubling situations that could recede into the background at Chagrin Falls but would come to the fore in New York: the fact that in Mexico he had not had the renewal of poetic creativity for which he had hoped; and, second, the painful awareness that alcohol, which he craved for its release from tension, induced behavior that he could not bear to recall. It was unfortunate that Lorna Dietz had written to him in Ohio about the episode with Katherine Anne Porter, thus removing his hope that this unsavory news would not have reached his New York friends, among whom K. A. was a great favorite. I know that K. A. had tried to limit the spread of this story, but there were others in Mexico who felt no qualms about repeating it. He wrote to Lorna that the subject had been "almost an obsession with me for the last month." So in New York he hid himself, and drank.

Once in his own house in Mixcoac he bounced back for a time, as his letters show. He arranged to do some reviewing for *Poetry;* went on an archaeological expedition to Tepoztlan, the first of several; formed a friendship with the young archaeologist; continued his reading; and went frequently to visit William Spratling in Taxco, where he became friendly with the painter David Siqueiros who painted his portrait. And he was writing some poetry, for a number of poems from this period are included in later collections. But most important of all was his pleasant social life with Peggy Baird and Lesley Simpson, with whom he enjoyed the delights of Mexico. On the whole, the swing was "up."

Taking Peggy under his protective wing undoubtedly helped, especially at a time when he did not feel haunted by financial worries. Bess had somehow arranged for money advances before the estate was settled. Peggy took things, and people, as they came; this was one of her charms to Hart. "A good sport" he had called her in a letter to Malcolm. Her ready forgiveness of an alcoholic tantrum had put him on his best behavior in order not to take advantage of her good nature. At that period Peggy had an elfin, fey quality, enhanced by her tiny physique and the unusual color of her eyes, which might be described as "dark yellow." Peggy had always been an undemanding dependent, rather like a well disposed child. Nobody expected her to earn a living —just to be herself. As a companion, this undemanding dependence appealed to Hart, making him feel "a man of substance." He took over the planning of Peggy's life, got her out of the unfavorable climate of Mexico City and settled her in the beneficent Taxco.

Something else may have had an effect on this growing intimacy, something I was not aware of until recently and about which I have heard no comment. I discovered that photographs taken when the two were about the same age show a marked facial resemblance between Peggy Baird and Grace Hart Crane — so much so that, on coming across a photograph labeled Grace Crane in the Columbia Crane Collection, my prompt reaction was that it had been mislabeled, that it was Peggy Baird. I had just been looking at photographs of Peggy taken with Hart in Mexico, when she was about the age of Grace Crane in the other photograph. I have known Peggy since the Twenties; I never saw Grace Crane. To those who knew them both it is probable that no resemblance would be seen. It is entirely facial, and likely to be more marked in photographs. In coloring and figure they were as unlike as in temperament. Grace Crane was a tall, blond, well-fleshed woman, not at all given to "taking things as they came." I doubt that Hart was consciously aware of any similarity.

Engaged in these friendly, unselfish pursuits, he was even able, for some time, to ride over discouraging news from the Crane estate lawyer: that the definite income he had thought assured could not be paid pending settlement of claims. But his "good stepmother" relieved his anxiety within a few weeks by again arranging a "money payment." With his last quarterly payment from the Guggenheim Foundation still to come, he could at least see some financial security in the months ahead. As yet it had not apparently entered his mind that there might be *no* assured income from the Crane estate.

It was in this state of general well-being that, a few days before Christmas, he took the bus to Taxco to spend the holidays with Peggy and to join the house-party about which he wrote to Malcolm.

Peggy's memoir tells about the relationship that began in Taxco, to the surprise of them both. In high spirits Hart planned with Peggy to leave on a kind of honeymoon tour, and returned to Mixcoac to sublet his house there, finish his review of Phelps Putnam's poems, and arrange his finances for the tour. He wired Peggy $75, and then wrote to her: "I'm in such a hectic rush ... dying now to be off to

Acapulco with you in two weeks' time, almost every moment must be bent to that end. . . . I can't do more than remind you that you already know the depth of my love for you." But his letter to Malcolm of January 9 tells only of his intention to leave Mixcoac; he leaves it to Peggy to write of the change in their relations, though he asks her: "Has Malcolm replied yet? Let me know when to write him if he hasn't."

Another subject that he doesn't mention to Malcolm, nor in letters to anybody else until February 8, is that he had started on a major poem in Taxco. Peggy's memoir has it that the birth of the poem and the love affair occurred simultaneously. Lesley Simpson recalled the poem's inception as occurring a little later, on January 27, also in Taxco, though his actual picture is much like Peggy's. It is difficult to pin down the exact time of the inception of a poem. Peggy recalls that Hart had worked on three stanzas during his New Year's visit. He had gone back to Taxco several times before Peggy had to give up her house there and move to his house in Mixcoac in the middle of February. Hart's correspondence shows that he had a rough draft of the entire poem by February 8 and that he did not regard the poem as finished until around March 20 to 25, when, as he later wrote to Zabel, he mailed a copy to *Poetry*. The creative "frenzy" that Simpson recalled as seizing the poet at dawn on January 27, in Taxco, can be taken as fact, it seems to me, as well as Peggy's recollection of its earlier start. Simpson's account was written in a letter to *The New English Weekly* shortly after Hart's death, with the aim of correcting Gorham Munson's impression that the poem had been composed several years earlier.

That the poetic stimulus had the same source as that which inspired his love seems likely. In early January he was writing to Peggy: ". . . I shall be with you certainly before next Sunday. I can and must say that your love is very precious to me. It seems to have given me an assurance that I thought long buried. You can give me many things besides — if time proves me fit to receive them: the independence of my mind and soul again, and perhaps a real wholeness to my body."

As to "bending every effort" to the end of getting away from Mixcoac and being off with Peggy, the plan was from the beginning impractical in Hart's unsettled state of finances. Unable to sublet, he had to give up the effort, substituting frequent visits to Taxco and luring her for stays of a week or so in Mixcoac. He had complicated his living arrangements there, largely to fight off loneliness, to the point at which he could not easily or quickly disentangle himself. He had permitted the American archaeologist to use his house as headquarters, where he came and went at will, between expeditions. He had installed Siqueiros and his family there, when the painter was being treated for a serious attack of malaria, and had also harbored some of Siqueiros' political associates who were subject to arrest or exile by the current administration. Some of them lingered even after the painter had left. Most serious of all, he had made a drinking companion of his servant Daniel with the result that Daniel's family, relatives, and friends had also taken over quarters. Who was master and who was man became uncertain. At times Hart actually feared Daniel, whose brothers were policemen; they could have made serious trouble for him for harboring political refugees. For a person of Hart's orderly habits, his neatness as to living conditions, there were daily exasperations. He could neither get rid of Daniel and his tribe nor put up with them. And his use of alcohol increased.

Yet he continued to work away at "The Broken Tower." By February 8 he was ready with a first draft, which he sent to Solomon Grunberg, writing him: "I am not, as you surmise, in a constant Bacchic state. Not by any means. However, I happen to be in something approximating it at this present moment, since I've got to work on the first impressive poem I've started on in the last two years." He went on to tell that he was in love again, "as never quite before," with a woman he had known for years, and "It has given me new perspectives, and, after many tears and groans — something of a reason for living." By February 13 he had made up his mind that he could not leave Mixcoac "until I get through some real work here," as he wrote to Peggy. He decided to let the troublesome domestic situation "ride."

By the time of his February 18 letter to Malcolm and Muriel, Peggy was living with him in Mixcoac, as the Cowleys knew, though Hart does not mention it. The letter is obviously a shy expression of thanks for their warm response.

He continued to enjoy his "conjugal life, however unofficial," as he wrote to a friend on March 10, then mentioned that he expected to receive "at least a portion of the yearly allowance left me by my father. . . . I'm just getting to work on a few things — and Peggy and I enjoy Mexico more than ever, being together." Then his stepmother wrote him discouraging news about her difficulties in settling the estate. "You're one of the finest people I've ever met," he wrote back to her, commiserating with her about her troubles and mourning his inability to help.

Financial uncertainty continued and caused him to suggest to Peggy that neither of them should "urge the other into anything but the most spontaneous and liberal arrangements." But he concluded: "I am bound to you more than I ever dreamed of being, and in the most pleasant and deep way . . . have wandered back to some of my early idealism."

He began to show signs of depending on Peggy to handle some of their problems, especially with Daniel. He was no longer the "man of substance." And at some point he began to resort to alcohol to sustain him, but without completely abandoning control as yet. His correspondence shows that he was still able to function normally; he finished "The Broken Tower" and mailed it first to Zabel and then to Malcolm. The accompanying letter contains his first direct and warm statement to Malcolm of his alliance with Peggy, in a tone that suggests continuance: "We're very happy together — and send you lots of love!"

Bess's letter was obviously meant as a warning, to prepare him for what was to come. For shortly after Easter an expected check failed to arrive, and Hart spent "feverish weeks running hither and yon every day or so to borrow enough money to keep us going until my check from the estate finally arrived" — so he wrote to Grunberg on April 12, though he still announced his and Peggy's intention to stay on in Mexico indefinitely. "If I can avoid drinking too much I'm expecting to get nearer solid earth than I have for several years. Sheer loneliness had nearly eaten me up. Peggy has sufficient sportsmanship, mentality, taste and sensuality to meet me on practically every level. And I think I'm learning considerable that would hardly be possible from any other person."

Then came news from the estate's lawyer that a suit against the Crane estate had stopped all advances; he let Hart know that for some time he had actually been depending on loans from his stepmother's own earnings.

That did it. Peggy's memoir describes the alcoholic madness that followed. For some days Hart was unable to make the necessary moves to leave Mexico. At last he wired Bess's man of business for enough to pay for passage home. They packed hastily and on April 24 were off for New York, again on the *Orizaba,* again with Captain Blackadder. Hart wrote to his stepmother of his intention to go on to Chagrin Falls, to help her run Canary Cottage. He does not mention to her any plan for Peggy. How could he?

To some extent, I think the lyric poet was a victim of the great depression as well as of his own temperament, somewhat on a par with the bankers and brokers who were throwing themselves out of windows. In spite of all his money worries and painful job hunts, over the years up until now he had had the sustaining thought that if worse came to worst there was a substantial fortune behind him. As Hart and Peggy took passage for New York, several branches of his father's business were entering bankruptcy. Added to this was his intense disappointment that he had received no word about "The Broken Tower." He never saw Malcolm's enthusiastic response, then in the mail.

His nerves were shattered by alcoholic excesses. His

life-long love for his mother had ended in hatred. He had uncalled-for doubts about his last poem. He was broke; so was the Crane estate; and so was the United States. Yet he had recently assumed an emotional responsibility such as he had always avoided. This was the prospect before him as the *Orizaba* sailed toward New York City from Havana.

The End

The Last Days
of Hart Crane

The seas all crossed,
weathered the capes, the voyage done . . .
Walt Whitman.

In the summer of 1931 I went to Mexico to get a divorce — a dismal journey for which I had little heart. A
good friend living in Mexico at the time was Hart Crane,
but he had been called home to Cleveland by his father's
death. He had written me from Cleveland, offering me his
house in Mixcoac — a suburb of Mexico City — with servants to take care of me until he returned. I was glad of his
absence, to tell the truth, being too maladjusted just then
to cope with his stormy temperament.

Instead, I stayed with Katherine Anne Porter, who also
had a house in Mixcoac, near Hart's, until she and her husband left for Europe. By that time I had found a place of my
own in Mexico City. Then I met Lesley Simpson, a professor of Spanish history, who relieved my loneliness by taking
me on long country walks and introducing me to a Mexico
of gaiety and fiestas I would never have discovered.

Hart Crane returned to Mexico, and he and I were delighted to see each other again. Hart represented to me the
family life I had just lost, making me no longer an exile.
And he felt much the same way about me. We were "home"
to each other, and both of us needed "home." Lesley and
Hart liked each other immediately, and the three of us spent
much time together. Lesley was as normal a man as I have
ever known. His mind was concerned with facts; all his
study was directed toward accuracy. Hart thought of himself as a homosexual, though almost without exception his
close friends were married couples. He kept his sex life apart

147

from his friendships. "Facts" were unimportant in his life and if confronted with such balderdash he would instantly roar it away. Passing ordinary people, he promptly clothed them in his own fantasy; they were pimps, cutthroats, prostitutes, *femmes fatales*, or princes in disguise.

"Look at that man, Peggy. Look at him, Lesley. See that line of his jaw. It's wonderful, something that Leonardo would have put on canvas. God, what form!"

A dull housewife would pass, her shopping bag on her arm.

"Just take a gander at that woman. A typical tart from the word go. Watch her mincing along on her way to a date, swishing her fanny. She's up to no good, you can see that!"

Such estimates of Hart's often got him into difficulties. One such detonated our first quarrel. Lesley had come by in the afternoon to take me out for a cocktail before dinner. As we were about to leave, loud, angry voices reached us from the patio. I murmured something to the effect that Hart must be in the vicinity. Lesley went out on the balcony to investigate, returned laughing.

"You guessed right. Hart's drunk and having a fuss with a taxi driver and the porter. I'll go down and see if I can stop the riot." I watched from the balcony. There was Hart, red-faced and angry, puffing portentously on his inseparable cigar. Behind him trailed his harried little Indian servant, Daniel, whom I knew well from my stay in Mixcoac. Hart was wearing a costume that I'm sure he thought of as that of a Mexican gentleman. White flannel trousers were surmounted by a brown and white serape and around his neck was a silver bridle — it had been worn by one of the conquistadors, of course. Perched jauntily on his head was one of the largest straw sombreros ever woven, tied under his chin by a multi-colored cord. Mexicans would judge that this gringo was satirizing the natives. No one in Mexico City, except the Indians coming in from the country, wears a native costume — which this wasn't. It could easily be looked upon as an insult.

Lesley returned, looking none too happy in his role as

a diplomat. Hart and Daniel were behind him. Hart was still sounding off about being overcharged by a thieving taxi driver. Daniel was plainly frightened. Lesley managed to tell me that he had succeeded in placating a very angry chauffeur, the house porter who tried to keep Hart from coming to my quarters, and two policemen who were about to take Hart to jail. It had taken a great deal of tact, plus cash, to get Hart and Daniel their liberty. I was anxious to get Hart out of my place as fast as possible, for he continued to make such an uproar that I feared I would be thrown out myself. Hart got the impression that I was on the side of the thief who had robbed him, which made me the object of his tirade. Lesley prevailed upon me to let Hart stay until things quieted down; in the dusk his costume wouldn't be so noticeable. Finally twilight came and Lesley led the two of them out. They made an unforgettable trio as I watched them through the courtyard — Hart with his sombrero bobbing on his head, a stream of smoke from his cigar, denouncing both me and the government without stopping; Lesley in his impeccable tweeds and Borsalino hat, making placating gestures; little Daniel flitting like a shadow in the rear. The next morning I received a telegram from Hart: "You can no longer consider yourself my friend."

Though outraged, I found it impossible to hold this attitude for long. If I accepted Hart as a person I had to accept his occasional wild extravagances. Soon the three of us were back on our old friendly basis. We roamed through the markets, buying pieces of blown glass or some tiny figurines, as if they were absolute necessities. Each scolded the others about extravagance, Lesley and I especially joining forces when Hart loaded himself down with an armful of flowers. We reminded him that he had a beautiful flower garden at Mixcoac. He just laughed at us.

"You will admit that I have no tuberoses or orchids, and they both last a long time, so there!"

My room being central, we usually met and returned there with our booty. The men frequently forgot their purchases, until every corner was piled high with knickknacks.

"Oh!" Hart would exclaim. "There's that virgin from Cho-
lula. I thought I'd left it on the bus."

But the climate of Mexico City did not agree with me.
I was troubled by constant colds. The brilliant sun gave me
no warmth. It became apparent that I must leave this high
altitude. Hart and Lesley were worried and nagged at me
to move where it was warmer. Then Bill Spratling came up
from Taxco, with news of a house near his that I could rent.
The three men insisted that I make the move. Here was a
house in a warm, even climate near someone I knew. Before
the evening was over I was scheduled to move to Taxco the
following week, and, without volition on my part, it was
also decided that I was to give a house party there over the
Christmas holidays. Hart and Lesley took all my affairs in
charge and Hart put me on the bus for Taxco.

The bus trip was hair-raising. On arrival I was met by
Bill and the owner of my house. They pointed it out to me
— a tiny white spot on the top of an inaccessible mountain,
with steps cut into the ascent. Only a goat can climb that,
I thought, but we got there, and I loved it. I inherited a
delightful servant, Maria Louisa, a little *mozo*, Jesus, as
well as various animals and birds.

Telegrams began to pour in from Hart. His house was
opposite a telegraph office and he often sent two telegrams
in as many hours. The poor messengers had to climb the
hill to my house, sometimes finding me without change for
a tip. All this led my small family to think it was a swain,
deeply in love, who spent the money on these messages.
Finally I climbed down the hill to the telegraph office and
sent a message to Hart to send me no more wires. I stopped
at the cantina to help bolster my nerve and strength for the
climb back. When I eventually arrived at my aerie, Maria
Louisa handed me another telegram from Hart, asking
simply: "Why not?"

Hart arrived two days before the rest of my guests, after
a barrage of letters and telegrams fixing and changing the
day and hour of his arrival. Still he was unexpected, having

appeared earlier than his last announcement. I was just finishing my morning bath when I heard Maria Louisa calling: "The senor comes! Hurry!" Sure enough, by the time I got to the veranda, there was Hart coming up the last turn, carrying his suitcase. I rushed down the precipitous steps to meet him. He dropped the suitcase and we embraced as if it had been years since we had seen each other. From the radiant faces of the maid and the gardener I could see it would be a waste of breath to make it clear he wasn't "mine" in their sense of the word. Hart will have the laugh of a lifetime, I thought, when I tell him what their sly, significant looks mean.

He was bubbling over with good humor and was entranced with the view from the veranda. At one moment it was a perfect Breughel and in the next it was painted by Grandma Moses. I called to Bill over the barranca, and asked him to have lunch with us, then showed Hart to his room, which always gave me a queasy feeling on entering, it was set so high over a deep barranca. Hart looked down and gasped.

"I see you expect your guests to be a sober lot. I give you leave to cut off my drinks when you think the next one will make me stagger."

We had a drink of rum into which I squeezed some drops of lime from my own tree. Hart said, over his drink: "Do sit me down at my typewriter tomorrow. I must finish a review for *Poetry*. But put my back to that town down below or it will never be done. I've never seen such a fascinating picture in my life. No wonder you are contented here. It is peace personified. . . ."

That hot day, Bill appeared carrying his Christmas present to me, a lovely pair of earrings, in the shape of a tiny basket, overflowing with flowers, made by a silversmith in a nearby village. The men insisted that I put them on immediately, so I went into my bedroom and changed into a dress that suited them. Hart whirled me around and stepped back to get the full effect.

"Isn't she wonderful, Bill? I'll fall in love with you," he said jokingly, and then, in a different tone, "Of course I really am already."

The three of us talked and drank far into the night — about the modern art of Mexico and how the Mexican artists were an integral part of their country. Bill finally left, refusing a nightcap, which Hart and I had after saying goodnight to him. We talked about the guests who were to arrive on Christmas Eve.

"I still can't take in that it's Christmas, without the traditional decorations," I said disconsolately. "The Christmas holidays need green, piles of it, and a brittle red."

"I'll find something in the morning. Don't worry. Mexico is wrapped in tinsel. You'll be surprised and satisfied. Just leave it to me. I'd better get to bed if I am to make good my boast."

Hart's Spanish was a hodge-podge of words strung together with gestures — an animated picture with sound. I came out on the porch the following morning to find myself at the end of just such a performance, with Maria Louisa and Jesus the audience. Hart's thick, short-cropped hair gleamed silver in the sun, his cigar in one hand making an arc. He was laughing heartily and, with his free hand, patting first one and then the other on the back. Evidently they had understood him, because they, too, laughed delightedly, clapping their hands like children.

"There's your coffee and orange juice, my dear," he said airily, after giving me a kiss. "Maria Louisa, Jesus and I are off to get your decorations. No, I'm not going to tell you what they will be. You can sit here cogitating on the subject. Anyway, it will be something red and green, which is what you asked for."

When they came staggering back up the steps, the effect may not have been Christmas, but the color was surely red and green. Each was loaded down with poinsettias that looked as heavy as cordwood — two hundred of them, about four feet long. In addition, Hart had twenty-five strange yellow blooms.

My other guests arrived on schedule, and we celebrated. My memory of the party is very slight, except that
there were musicians who attempted to drown out the noise
of the cathedral bells.

After seeing everyone off on the bus, Hart and I sat
down for a quiet drink in the cantina, deciding that we had
had quite enough of the holiday spirit and celebration. We
would both stay in our eagle's nest and work hard during the
rest of his stay. No more drinking and parties. Making that
pre-New Year's resolution, we soberly climbed up to the
house.

The cathedral bells had been ringing all the time we
were in the Plaza, but on the patio they were deafening. Every so often they would stop for a second, when a fresh man
relieved the bell ringer. The noise reverberated around the
house angrily. To me it was terrifying. Maria Louisa
proudly told us that the men would be able to keep it up for
the next ten days!

"It can't last," Hart yelled at me over the dinner table.
From then on we communicated mainly by signs. There
were to be fireworks and dancing in the Plaza. We might as
well go. Anything to get away from the clamor of the cathedral bells. The noise was nowhere near as harsh down in the
town, being above us rather than in our ears. The fireworks
were gay and exciting. We danced until we could dance no
longer, then stopped for a drink and back again. Everything
appeared to be spinning off into an infinity of color and
music.

"It's all a poem and I shall write it, with us right in the
middle of it, darling."

That night, or what was left of it, we slept in my bed,
the clamor of the bells our wedding music. The next morning Maria Louisa knocked at my room before bringing us
our coffee and orange juice. She had never done this before.
Somehow it showed us she put an official seal on our union.
The bells were still monotonously flailing the air. We were
so wrapped up in each other, so ludicrously happy, that we
hardly noticed. Hart was drunk in the excitement of the

moment, a bit awed, but still unafraid. He kept looking at me and laughing.

"I don't believe it for a moment, darling, but be good and tell me that it's not a figment of my imagination."

Teasing, I asked if he thought he could concentrate on writing the poem. And so he began, phrases scribbled on paper, voiced in words to test the sound, discarded completely, or held for a later trial. He was the instrument on which he played the words, changing each perhaps a hundred times before retaining one small fragment. Actually, he didn't mind the noise; he frequently kept his phonograph going full blast while he was at work.

This went on for three days, with little or no respite, and finally he had rough drafts of three stanzas. He was in love and wanted me with him every moment. I was as necessary as the bells which seemed to clarify his thought. His energy seemed inexhaustible. He was keyed to the highest pitch. Yet this experience was somewhat frightening to him. I, too, was more than a little disturbed. He had confided to me that for some time he had feared that he would never again feel the urge to write, and now he was again writing poetry. He had found something beyond sensuality, he felt purified of a sense of guilt which he had always had as a homosexual.

The poem was not yet finished but Hart began to feel that he must get back to his house in Mixcoac. There would be a pile of mail and he was anxious to hear about the settling of his father's estate. At one time Mr. Clarence Crane had been rated a millionaire, but for years there had been business reverses and at the time of his death there was some doubt that the estate would cover the incurred debts. Hart hoped that inside a week he could answer his letters, write a promised review, and finish the poem. Then he wanted to take a short trip or two with me, the first to Acapulco. He would come down to Taxco, stay with me overnight, then we would set out the next day. I was willing to go as far as Acapulco, but I was very contented where I was and had no desire to ramble uncomfortably around the country. I liked the idea of a short separation. It was hard to keep up with his fierce tempo, charging everything with tremendous energy, drinking, writing, making love, and just enjoying himself. It was like living with an erupting volcano.

Knowing Hart would return, I found it lovely to sit alone drinking my coffee, looking at the sun touching the brown mountains honeycombed with abandoned silver mines. Sounds rose up softly from the town below. The Christmas fiestas were over, and it was quiet again. Then one mid-afternoon, bells rang at once in all the churches, rockets zoomed right and left, and there was Maria Louisa dressed in her best, anxious to get down and mingle in the excitement. It seemed to me there were only a few days between the end of the Christmas festivities and this new uproar. I asked her what this was all about.

"Why this is very important. It is the name day of our saint." She got as far as the lime tree and then raced back laughing.

"The senor is coming! He is right here."

There was Hart, close on her heels, and I hadn't expected to see him for another week. It was such a delightful surprise that I forgot completely that only a few hours ago it had seemed that being alone and without noise was something to be desired.

"I just couldn't stay away, darling. Are the bells still ringing, or did you order this as a welcome for me?"

He had written another stanza of the poem and it was beginning to show that it would be equal to the best of his work. I was filled with pride when he said it had been written to me, though I thought this was probably lover's license.

"We will now go and celebrate our saint's name day, whoever that may be, and we won't forget Bacchus."

Late in the night, while the rest of Taxco still whirled, we climbed the steps back to the house. Hart then showed me a letter from his family lawyer, preparing him to expect little from his father's estate. Late in life, his father had started his third wife in a lucrative business of her own.

They had taken a large house in Chagrin Falls, outside of Cleveland, and converted part of it into a restaurant with collected American antiques. It was successful from the start, wealthy women using it for card clubs and business men for banquets.

"We must stay there for a while when we get back. You and Bess will love each other. I've already written her that I will be married by the time she sees me."

I could see that he still expected to inherit enough to live on, however modestly, for his only concern was whether I would be willing to live in Mexico, or some place equally cheap, rather than in New York where we would have to pinch and budget. "Anyway, you were never well in New York. In the short time you've been here in Taxco you look healthier than in all the years I've known you. Perhaps some of that is due to my love. You might let me think so, anyway."

The following day, while we sat over late coffee, Maria-Louisa went into a long tale of something that was to happen that very day. We gathered there was to be another fiesta and we must hurry so that we wouldn't miss anything.

"No more dancing and no more music," Hart teased her, "or you and Jesus will have to carry me up every one of those infernal steps." She made the sign of the cross, giggling, and ran off. "Something we must see, evidently. Get your best clothes on. I think we're in for a rodeo," Hart said, roaring with laughter.

When we got to the Plaza, the whole town was moving en masse toward the town entrance. We were at the tail end of the crowd, so it was some time before we realized that a procession was forming. Everyone was carrying or leading an animal or a bird, including the children. But what a metamorphosis had taken place in the animal kingdom! The horses looked like something out of a circus, with gilded hoofs, collars of gold paper, and brushed so that their coats could have been a demonstration for hair tonic, manes and tails as if marcelled by a fancy barber. Paints and dyes had been used profusely. It was somewhat strange to see a grass-green pig go grunting by, led on a purple ribbon. One white cat had been dyed pink in blotches, which she was trying to wash off, cat-fashion; she was also unaccustomed to wearing earrings. Green parrots were turned blue and blue ones green, while a white cockatoo was completely silvered. Not to be outdone, there was Maria Louisa carrying our tomorrow's meal, a turkey, with strands of tiny silvered Christmas beads wound around its neck, at which it was pecking vigorously.

We clung to each other and looked in awe. The procession was moving toward one of the outlying small churches and there was a priest, solemnly blessing each bird and beast as they passed in front of him.

"Whores, dressed up for an Easter parade," Hart whispered. Just then my eye caught sight of a bull attempting to mount a stolid cow. I quickly dragged Hart away from the crowd, afraid he would let out one of his full-throated laughs that would end the solemnity of the occasion once and for all.

One evening, shortly after this, Hart went down to the town alone. Some time later a tiny *mozo* came up the hill and handed me a note. "Your friend got in some kind of scrape and is now in jail." I talked to Bill Spratling, and he told me Hart would simply have to stay in jail for the night. I was angry and hurt; this left me in an unsavory situation. I knew he had been outrageous to many of his friends, but he had insisted that I was the woman he loved and wanted to marry. I didn't go to see him the next day, nor did I see him off on the bus, which he took that afternoon. Bill came over and attempted an explanation.

"Anyone who gets drunk publicly in Mexico is apt to land in jail. It's a means of increasing the town's finances. Because Hart is a foreigner he had to pay nearly three times as much as my house boy. Hart thinks you are acting high hat."

I never did find out what he had done, but it could have been nothing important: a too-loud voice, or solo dancing in the street. From anything worse there would have been reverberations. But he never apologized for this or any of his other arrests. They were affronts to his dignity. It never entered his head that I was in any way affected. That I was already in an unconventional position, made no pleasanter by notoriety, didn't occur to him.

As soon as he reached Mixcoac, he started a campaign to get me there. He was having trouble with Daniel, he wrote. Daniel was getting drunk every day and threatening him with knives and revolvers. I was to be the oil on the troubled waters. Daniel had great respect for me and would quiet down with me in the house. Knowing Daniel, I thought it an unlikely story. But, though it was a ruse, I was willing to make the change for a few days. We arranged to meet at the *Broadway*, our favorite restaurant. He met me in high spirits with a corsage of orchids. Sweet peas were on the table and cocktails miraculously appeared as I stepped in the door.

"I'm so glad to have you here, dear. It isn't so bad at the house as I pictured, but I thought if I made it strong enough you'd come armed to the teeth to protect me. The servants are delighted at a visit from the senora. I left Daniel sweeping and dusting like a mad Dutch housewife. He's going over to the General's garden for some flowers to decorate the house." He laughed gleefully, pleased as a child who successfully pulls off a trick. And so was I.

"I've got an idea that might amuse us this afternoon," he said after lunch. "There's an old Charlie Chaplin picture in town and I thought we might go." The taxi driver looked at us curiously when Hart told him where we wanted to go. The streets became narrower, showing poverty and deprivation — low, patched-up adobe houses roofed with flattened tin cans, people wearing tattered, dirty clothing. The driver stopped. Hart looked around and said, "Shall we take a chance?" Having come so far, we decided to go into the unprepossessing theatre. Never have I felt more conspicuous than when I walked down that aisle, conscious of the orchids on my shoulder. And there was Hart in an immaculate white linen suit, a gardenia in his button-hole and carrying a box of Huyler's candy he had bought for me. Everyone in the audience turned to stare at us silently, as if their heads moved on well-oiled pivots. I felt foolish and tugged at Hart's hand. "We can't leave now. What a stink of ancient piss!" he said. But when Charlie came on the screen everything else was forgotten, both by the audience and us. Tears streamed down our faces and we clung to each other laughing louder than anyone else in the house. The greatest mime of the century had brought the orchids and rags together in joint appreciation.

Back at Hart's house in Mixcoac, there was no evidence of the disorder he had described so vividly. His lovely large room, uncluttered by too much furniture, was dominated by the revealing portrait of Hart painted by David Alfaro Siqueiros. It showed him reading, the luminous light focused on his silver hair. There were vases of flowers in every room, sheaves of wheat and flowers hanging on the walls. Beneath the graceful cordiality with which Daniel and his wife greeted me, I sensed also a great relief at my presence.

Our quarters were three large rooms. The servants were officially only Daniel and his wife, but there were loads of relatives clustering around. Besides all the other animals one finds around every Mexican house, Hart had bought me a tiny white kid. Intended for a future meal, in twenty-four hours it became a pet with everyone. If it found itself alone, it would run around bleating for attention, its tiny hoofs clicking like a woman's high heels on the tiled floors. I insisted that the kid be given away before it became an even closer member of the family. I pointed out that the Fernandez family (Daniel's) were slavering at the mouth, waiting for it to be table fare. "Oh, no, dear, it's yours. Daniel wouldn't dare touch it without first consulting you," Hart demurred. He said that I would be leaving him in a few days and returning to Taxco and would therefore be present neither at the slaughter nor feast. I knew that once the cute mite had waked him in the morning, nuzzling his face with its cold nose, he would want no part of its flesh on his table. The last I saw of the kid Daniel was leading it out of the grilled iron gate and wiping the tears from his eyes with his free hand.

"Crocodile tears," Hart scoffed. "He's giving it to some member of his family and in about two weeks I'll be asked if he can't have a day off to go to his grandmother's funeral."

I stayed a week or so with Hart at Mixcoac and every minute was filled to the brim. Lesley Simpson's wife had joined him and all of us were together frequently. I would have my coffee and orange juice in bed, Hart — always an early riser — bringing it in triumphantly. He bought me an onyx ring and I bought a hat to meet his need of conventionality. We would climb to the roof of his house (vine-covered, with blossoms blue as the sky) from which there was a wonderful view of Popocatepetl. Still, I wanted to go back to Taxco.

Taxco was as soft as an eiderdown quilt after the plateau chill of Mexico City. For the moment the bells were silent, there was a paucity of fiestas, and there was attentive Maria Louisa. My mind and body lapped up the peaceful relaxation.

True, I knew by now I loved Hart. But the high tension by which he lived was exhausting, and I was fatigued. I tried to think over our future relationship, which meant accepting his tremendous vitality. To think of changing him would be as absurd as trying to change the course of a hurricane. Moreover, I loved him for those very qualities which I feared to live with. But I ended by giving myself up to the devotion of the sun, luxuriating in slothfulness with a mirage of hope.

This fine state was doomed to end, but this time it was not precipitated by Hart. The owner of my house had sold it *in absentia,* and the new owner now appeared to take possession — politely but persistently. I had a faint acquaintance with the new owner and wished to have no trouble, so I got out as fast as possible. Friends put me up while we made inquiries about another house. Another guest was already on the scene, the well-known, no-longer-young poet W. B. By now my love affair with Hart was well publicized, and our intention to marry. W. B. made it clear he didn't like Hart personally nor the poetry he had written so far. But, he said at length, if Hart were left to his normal inclinations he might become a real poet. So I was responsible for Hart's dereliction, and I should accept the responsibility for the effects.

Hart had been writing to me to come to Mixcoac and, since no house was to be had in Taxco, I agreed to do so. Much as I wished to be with him, I would have preferred it on my own grounds — in Taxco, which we both loved.

Hart had been lonely, I could see. He had done everything to make me comfortable in Mixcoac, fixing up the extra room so that I could work at my painting. An old friend of ours, Marsden Hartley, was in Mexico City and he came out nearly every afternoon. The three of us walked and talked and discussed Hart's poetry. It was a sober, quiet period. I remember Hart's saying: "I'll make you a good husband yet. Nothing ostentatious. It will be a paltry thing but my own."

One sunny afternoon we sat on the porch reading — a large glass pitcher of beer at hand, comfortable in pillows and serapes, books, my cigarettes, Hart's cigars. We grinned companionably. "We won't move the entire afternoon," I said firmly. "Complete relaxation, my dear," he said. "We have it too seldom."

It was good to see him in this unusual state of tranquility. If only he could make such moods spontaneous acts of his own. Now, propped up with pillows, his back against the house, engrossed in his book, he looked indeed like the fine portrait by Siqueiros hanging on the wall inside.

Then a taxi stopped in front of the house. Two women. When we recognized who they were — Claire Smith and Bill Seabrook's first wife — we both let out a call of welcome and ran to the gate to meet them. We insisted they spend the afternoon and have dinner with us. Daniel was sent rushing for limes and other supplies, and we soon had them supplied with drinks of tequila, which, all agreed, was no worse than bootleg liquor in the States. Hart tactfully left me with Claire while he showed Kate over the house, for Claire had obviously been surprised to find me living there with him. Then he returned with Kate and did the same job for Claire — an entrancingly beautiful woman and a gifted writer — while Kate and I discussed our divorces. It turned out to be a delightful interlude, a bit of home fare, and Hart responded to it as such.

Disheartening letters arrived from Cleveland. Hart at last realized he could expect nothing from his father's estate. His stepmother offered us a haven in Chagrin Falls, or a small amount of money each month from her own pocket, which Hart felt he had no right to accept. It was a festering sore that he couldn't make a living from his poetry. Subsidies for poets were then few. Money for book reviews is meager at best and in his case even more so because of the time he spent over them.

The Broken Tower had been finished after several months of concentrated work, and had been sent to *Poetry*. No comment in reply; afterwards I learned that the manuscript had been lost in the mail. Hart began to doubt his judgment and his ability as a poet. This was the only long piece he had finished in the time he had been in Mexico. His desperation at the silence of editors and financial insecurity began to mount and along with it his daily consumption of alcohol. He kept referring to himself as "a rat in a trap." Moroseness and anger against the world possessed him. He became an ugly, sick man in mind and body. Constant tirades against the servants, Mexico, his friends in the States. When he was put in jail for being drunk on the streets, it was a conspiracy to ruin his reputation. He would offer to set me free at one moment and in the next he feared I would take him at his word.

"Stay with me, dear. I need you so. Try to forgive my raving moments."

During those days we saw no one. Lesley Simpson, the only person from whom he might have taken advice, was out of town. I urged him to go back to Cleveland, thinking a different environment might straighten him out. In his saner moments he agreed and even at times became enthusiastic.

"You and Bess will get on first rate. She's a wonderful person. It will be monotonous but there is plenty of good music to be heard in Cleveland, good plays, too. I'll get off a letter today."

But no letter would be written; he didn't have the power to sit down and use the typewriter — to concentrate for any time on a thought. He was possessed by a demon that gave him no peace.

One day I decided, in desperation, to ask Mary Doherty and our friend Louise to come out for dinner. Hart liked both the girls and it might take his mind off his troubles. Mary was secretary to the head of the Mexican Department of Public Welfare, and an old hand at Mexican affairs. Hart was delighted with the idea.

"Good! You're too much alone with me. I'm letting you have my blackest moods. Company is just what we need."

But when I got up the Sunday I expected the girls, he was already drunk. He was still in his pajamas, a serape flung over his shoulder, and he followed me in that costume wherever I went, so I couldn't telephone them not to come. He was wild, talking to himself incoherently. When the girls arrived, they were horrified. They were afraid to go away and leave me there alone. Hart was worse than I had ever seen him. His speech jumbled together so that we couldn't understand him most of the time. He was in a torrent of rage, with no special object we could detect — stumbling from room to room. Suddenly he stopped before the Siqueiros portrait, which normally he admired greatly. He flung out his hand, pointing at it with a gesture of disgust, and his enunciation became clearer: "Look at that piece of trash!" He laughed derisively. "One of Mexico's greatest painters! What a travesty! Do you think that jackal will be known ten years after he dies? Why, that picture hasn't been painted a year and the paint is already cracking. It's a daub executed with house paint!" He glared at us, demanding agreement. "Do you think I'll take that back to the States and become a laughing stock — gulled into buying that piece of junk? By God, I'll get rid of it this very minute. It's disgraced my walls long enough."

In a flash, there was an old-fashioned straight razor in his hand and he was before the canvas, hand lifted ready to strike. We cried out and ran to him, trying to hold his arm, but he flung us off as if we were leaves. There was the sharp sound of ripping canvas. Then he flung the razor into a corner and rushed out of the room.

"Something must be done. He's dangerous." It was Mary.

Daniel had disappeared — escaping Hart's violence. After a few moments of futile discussion, we heard Hart summon us peremptorily into the front room.

"I want Mary and Louise to witness this." Hart was sitting at his desk and he spoke calmly. "It is my last will. Read it. I'm leaving everything to Peggy except a few trinkets for Bess and Zell. Peggy is the only person with faith in me and my ability as a poet."* He signed the will and gave it to Mary, asking her to keep it safe. "There, I wanted to get that done, because this afternoon I am going to kill myself." The statement was made in an even, steady voice.

He again began pacing from one room to another, saying nothing. Once he appeared with a glass of liquor in his hand, and a bit later there was a crash of glass as if he had thrown it on the tiled floor. We scarcely moved and hardly dared to talk. Suddenly he was with us again, this time holding a small bottle of iodine. He waved it before us, but craftily just out of reach.

---

*This, of course, was not true. Malcolm Cowley, then on the staff of The New Republic, had written to Hart praising The Broken Tower highly, and Hart respected his judgment; but the Letter had not arrived. The delay in hearing from Poetry was not unusual, as I had tried to make him see. It was self-doubt that was preying on his mind, which demanded constant reassurance — something not to be had. — P. B.

164

"Fools! You thought I didn't mean to kill myself, but I am a man of integrity at least."

We attempted cajoling him, as if he were a child with a dangerous toy, at the same time relieved it wasn't the razor. He knew we would let him come to no harm, for he could have chosen a different spot, but he held his audience for the melodrama. When he lifted the bottle to his lips, I grabbed his arm. A few drops spilled on his lips, the rest falling on his chin and the serape.

Then the little figure of Daniel appeared in the doorway, his eyes filled with apprehension. Mary ordered him to get a doctor and he disappeared in a flash. The doctor proved to be a competent man with a great deal of understanding. He put Hart to sleep with an injection. Hart's lips were burned a trifle, the doctor said, but he thought he would be all right in the morning. Someone must stay near him all night, and if he wakened, give him one of the sleeping tablets which the doctor left with us. He took down all our histories, Mary reeling them off in Spanish. Then he pocketed his fee, shook hands all around, and left. Daniel went to make us some sandwiches, and the three of us settled down in the front room.

"You must get him back to the States as soon as possible," Mary said firmly. I replied that, whether or not Hart agreed to go, surely I was going. "I'm not sure you will be permitted to go without him," Mary said. "The doctor will have to make a report about this. On account of Hart's former arrests, I am inclined to think the authorities will take this seriously. Attempted suicide is a jail offense here — the old Catholic ruling. And you are as good as married to Hart."

This was grim and stunning news. I said I would try to get him out as soon as possible, and she thought the authorities would place no obstructions.

Hart woke once during the night and asked for water, saying he was burning up. I gave him some, with the sleeping tablet, and he fell into the first relaxed sleep he had had for days. Daniel took my place toward morning. I rested for a while, and as I was having my coffee Hart called to me, saying he was hungry. I was glad to see he was willing to stay in bed for the day, and, with his old laugh, he said he was being pampered.

I couldn't tell what he remembered of the day before except that a doctor had been called, though he looked like a whipped pup. Everything had piled up on him, he said. "A touch of tequila might have had something to do with it," he admitted. I broached the subject of our going home as fast as possible, and he agreed. In fact he thought that part of his upset was that he hadn't gotten that letter off to the States.

In less than a week our passage money arrived by telegraph. It was delivered to us in the form of silver *tostons,* each about the size and weight of a fifty-cent piece, in sturdy canvas sacks which were thrown negligently on the floor of our taxi. We used them as a resting place for our feet on our way into Mexico City to pay for our passage home. It gave us a festive feeling to step on that amount of currency. Our first stop was at the Ward Line, where we found that the *Orizaba* was to sail in a few days. We made reservations and Hart requisitioned half a dozen small tots to carry in our money sacks in payment. Then we ran into trouble. The Ward Line, in accordance with a recent edict, could not change more than twenty *tostons* a day into foreign currency. The clerk could do nothing. He sent us to the Bank of Mexico with our sacks.

There, more little boys were engaged to carry in the money. It was indecorously dumped on the floor in front of a cashier's window. Hart was beginning to be restive, so I suggested he do some last-minute shopping and leave this business to me. We arranged to meet for lunch.

The laborious process of counting the *tostons* was started, and then the bank closed for the protracted lunch period. At this rate, I would never meet the deadline to pay for passage. Resolving to keep this problem a secret, I met Hart and found him bubbling over with good humor about his purchases, all of which he considered great bargains. Knowing that he tired easily after that exhausting weekend, I persuaded him to take a taxi back to Mixcoac. I added that I might not be back at dinner time; I wanted to see some friends in Mexico City after I got the steamship tickets.

Back at the bank, I found the money still lying on the floor. I had only two hours, but the cashier explained to me firmly and politely that he could not deliver the American money to me until he had finished counting it, in spite of my receipt showing the amount sent to me. I made ominous references to the American Embassy, and was finally informed I would have an audience with the President of the Bank. Two soldiers conducted me down a long corridor and we stopped at a massive door which, when opened, revealed two new soldiers to whom I was turned over. It felt more like an arrest than an audience. We entered a long, long room, covered with a heavy carpet. At the end of the room was a massive desk, to which I was marched. Here were two new, grim warriors, taking the place of my last escorts. It was only then that I realized the man facing me behind the desk, with hard obsidian eyes, was none other than Plutarco Calles, once the President of all Mexico and still the power behind the throne.

Without a word, he handed over a slip of paper, bowed, and smiled slightly at my stammered thanks.

When I handed the cashier the slip of paper from Calles, the money was waiting for me. There was just time to make the Ward Line office.

I had a few drinks with my friends Carleton and Betty Beals; then the three of us taxied to Mixcoac to pick up Hart and have dinner in town. An excited Daniel ran out of the gate to meet us. Rapid Spanish followed between Carleton and Daniel. My heart sank. The story was that Hart, after arriving home, had done some packing, written a few letters, and then had started to worry about me. By nightfall he had me robbed, raped and left for dead along the wayside. Yes, he had had a drink or two but Daniel insisted that he wasn't the least bit drunk. He had gone into the city to report my disappearance to the police! We sat and waited some time for Hart, but the Beals got hungry and left.

Hart finally arrived, angry, chiefly at finding me safe and sound, money, tickets, and virtue intact. He had insisted on having one of the attaches at the American Embassy accompany him to the official radio station to broadcast my description! And I hadn't even been late in returning. Hart continued to fret and fume, going back again to *The Broken Tower*. It wasn't any good, nobody liked it, he was finished as a poet.

That night I lay awake a long time. What on earth could help this tortured soul? I would insist on complete rest and doctor's care as soon as we got to New York. . . . Yet, the following morning he was full of gaiety. We finished packing, and the trunks went off.

That afternoon, our last, we gave a cocktail party at the *Broadway*. Such a nice lot of people! I hated the thought of leaving. Everyone cheered and toasted us when Hart, in fine good humor, announced we were to be married in New York and would return in two years. Then he took me for a farewell sight of our favorite market and he bought me a corsage large enough to satisfy a Hollywood queen. For the time being I was able to forget all problems. The next day the taxi was at the door long before we were ready. At long last, Daniel squeezed us into the car, tears streaming down his cheeks as he put an armful of flowers on our laps, this time from our garden, not the General's.

"We will come back here," Hart said as we drove off. "If we're delayed, we must send for Daniel and the family. I won't have a life without them."

Vera Cruz was hot that day in July, and it was pleasant to go aboard the *Orizaba*. This was Hart's second trip on this ship, and he was acquainted with many of the officers, to whom he promptly introduced me. I noted some raised eyebrows among the uniformed men when Hart informed them of our marriage in the near future. We were to reach Havana in the morning and have the whole day ashore. At the dinner table we planned what we should do. Hart knew and loved the city, having been there frequently when he had lived on the Isle of Pines. He wanted to spend most of the day showing me the sights. My shopping wouldn't take much time.

"I know a restaurant where they speak English. You go there as soon as you're through, and every so often I'll stop by to see if you've arrived." He stopped, a trifle embarrassed. "If you are worried, I promise not to take a drink until you arrive." Here was a new Hart, full of vigor and strength. He began to look and plan ahead, and this time with some sense of reality. He was trying to fit me into his picture, making it logical. He decided we should stay in New York only a few days. He wanted to see his publisher. For my part, I would have to go to the country to see about my house. We would stay at the Hotel Lafayette while in New York.

"I'll wire for rooms in the morning. It will be a nice place for a brief honeymoon. Your divorce papers should be there by then, and we can get married immediately. I've given you a hard time with my wildness. Perhaps I can make it up to some extent. Cleveland I can take if you are with me. It won't be for long."

We stayed in my cabin all night and were awake to see Morro Castle slide past the porthole in the early morning. We had a comfortable breakfast aboard ship. The city was fresh and brittle in the morning sun. Hart pointed out the restaurant where we were to meet, cautioning me not to go down side streets and get lost. My purchases were made in a short time. On my way to the restaurant I stopped in a music store and bought a few records as a surprise for Hart. By then I was carrying quite a load. I dropped my bundles in the long, cool room of the restaurant, which was empty, confident I was in the right place although the waiter spoke no English and I could not find out if Hart had been there. After eating a sandwich, I began to look anxiously at the clock. The boat was to sail at four-thirty. At last the waiter led a man to my table who spoke English. No, there had been no man answering to Hart's description in the place. Finally, with the aid of the waiter, I ordered a cab and gathered up my bundles.

A perturbed purser met me at the top of the gangplank. "Mr. Crane is worried about you. He has been on the ship for over an hour." Several other persons stopped me and said the same thing. I was in no mood to hear excuses from him. I dumped my packages on the bed, washed, and changed my clothes for dinner. Hart, I thought, could be found at the bar — the explanation that I had finally arrived at for his failure to turn up at the restaurant. I would take some of the new records there, play them on the phonograph near the bar, and listen to them over a highball.

The bartender gave me my drink and told me that Hart had been looking for me, adding that he had had a few drinks. I started one of my new records. My drink beside me, I opened a package of matches to light a cigarette. There was a swift explosion. The box of Cuban matches had exploded and the flame ran around my hand and up my arm. I knew only dimly that the bartender had picked me up and I heard him say to someone: "Burned, badly." I came to, in pain, in the doctor's office. He was wrapping my arm in a solution of tannic acid. Then Hart arrived, noisily. He ranted about my carelessness, and how awkward I was for such a small person. The doctor ordered him to leave and come back for me in an hour. He gave me a large drink of straight whiskey, and said I would be put to bed with a sleeping tablet that should keep me asleep until morning.

Hart reappeared at intervals before the doctor was ready to let me go. He was threatening to sue the match company or the ship itself for negligence. The doctor plainly resented his intrusions, as did I. The last time he arrived the doctor had just finished his work and was giving me medicine in a glass. "This will take effect by the time she gets to bed. I'll look in on her later," he said to Hart. Hart tried to carry me from the doctor's office, but I resisted this, and groped along the wall. There was my cabin at last, I was in bed, and I was out.

It may have been an hour, or only fifteen minutes, later; Hart was again in the room, asking questions and demanding answers. I begged to be left alone. It happened again and again. Once the doctor was with him, and he gave me something to drink. I sensed a mounting hysteria in the voice that was Hart's, but I could not get up. Then came a different, quiet voice in the room, from someone leaning over me.

"Will you give me authority to lock Mr. Crane in his cabin?"

Why hadn't this been thought of before? With my last strength I begged the voice to do just that. I was barely awake enough to hear that Hart was being urged to his room; with a little sleep I would be able to take care of things in the morning.

I woke up in broad daylight, rang for the stewardess, and asked for coffee. She helped me into a housecoat and went with me to the infirmary. My arm was throbbing. The doctor dressed it and said nothing about Hart's conduct the night before. Had I imagined it? I wondered. Hart appeared in my room, on my heels, sober but nervous, and, I thought, frightened. He told me he recalled nothing of the previous evening after first seeing me in the doctor's office. His wallet and a ring were missing. I went with him to his room, to see if they could be found, although he was sure they had been stolen. He needed a drink immediately, he said, and I agreed, but insisted he eat some breakfast and I rang for a steward, who quickly brought a menu and Hart ordered a large meal. He said he had not begun to drink the day before until he got back on the ship. I had been waiting in the wrong restaurant. As soon as the tray was placed in front of him he began to devour the food; he had not eaten dinner the previous night. I asked him to dress and meet me in my cabin, where the stewardess was waiting for me.

She brushed my hair and helped me into a dress that would go over my heavy bandage. Then Hart came in and sat beside me on my berth. He was still in his pajamas, wearing a light topcoat for a robe. I asked him to shave and dress.

"I'm not going to make it, dear. I'm utterly disgraced."

Perhaps some glimmering of his actions the night before had come to haunt him, beyond the loss of the ring and the pocketbook. If so, he gave me no hint. The loss of his wallet, containing most of his money, was upsetting. It would be embarrassing to ask for more as soon as we set foot in New York. It was a delicate problem but not too serious. He was always immaculate and I kept insisting that he would feel in a calmer mood and more self-possessed once he was dressed in clean clothes.

"All right, dear. Good-bye."

The door closed, and the stewardess finished dressing me. She made no comment on my caller; apparently she had detected nothing startling. She asked what I would like for lunch.

Then the ship's whistle gave a loud blast. The boat shuddered and came to a standstill. In that horrifying second I knew it was Hart. I don't think I heard the cries of "Man Overboard." Running to the lower deck with the stewardess, I remember clutching her starched white sleeve. The first lifeboats were just being lowered. In one, passing me, there was the doctor. I was unable to move for a time. I was willing Hart back with all my might, to stand beside me, laughing at my silly fears. Someone came up and said something to me that had to be repeated.

"The Captain requests that you come to the bridge." I followed the officer automatically.

I passed a blur of faces — stairs to climb one after another — a hand guiding me. Then I was standing alone with someone who must be the Captain.

He brought me out of my shock. From his lips came a stream of furious profanity. Every so often, as if to catch his breath, he would turn his back and growl: "Twenty-six years at sea, and this happens to me for the first time." Then the oaths again. Occasionally he looked out at the flat Caribbean through binoculars. Once he took them from his eyes and said: "If the propellers didn't grind him to mincemeat, then the sharks got him immediately."

I looked out on the sea, following his gaze. Not a ripple. Like a mirror that could be walked on. The tiny boats, still far off, were coming nearer. There was no good news or there would have been some signal and the Captain would have stopped spewing obscenities. No sign of the gay tempestuous poet, driven to this end which surely he had never meant. It had been a threat — to get a reaction — like the iodine in Mixcoac. I don't know how long I looked out over the water — Hart's grave.

The lifeboats bumped softly against the side of the ship and there was the noise of winches. The engines started turning and the boat picked up speed. Alone, I stumbled down the steep iron stairs. It was high noon.

Letters of Hart Crane

Letters of Others